THE HISTORY OF CIVILIZATION

SOCIAL ORGANIZATION

THE HISTORY OF CIVILIZATION

General Editor C. K. Ogden

The *History of Civilization* is a landmark in early twentieth Century publishing. The aim of the general editor, C. K. Ogden, was to "summarise in one comprehensive synthesis the most recent findings and theories of historians, anthropologists, archaeologists, sociologists and all conscientious students of civilization." The *History,* which includes titles in the French series *L'Evolution de l'Humanité*, was published at a formative time in the development of the social sciences, and during a period of significant historical discoveries.

A list of the titles in the series can be found at the end of this book.

SOCIAL ORGANIZATION

W H R Rivers

London and New York

First published in 1924 by Routledge, Trench, Trubner
Reprinted in 1996, 1998, 1999 by Routledge
2 Park Square, Milton Park, Abingdon, Oxfordshire OX14 4RN
711 Third Avenue, New York, NY 10017
First issued in paperback 2014
Routledge is an imprint of the Taylor and Francis Group, an informa business

Transferred to Digital Printing 2008

© 1996 Routledge

British Cataloguing in Publication Data

ISBN 978-0-415-15572-4 (hbk)
ISBN 978-0-415-86799-3 (pbk)

ISBN Pre-history (12 volume set): 978-0-415-15611-4
ISBN History of Civilization (50 volume set): 978-0-415-14380-2

Publisher's Note
The publisher has gone to great lengths to ensure the
quality of this reprint but points out that some
imperfections in the original may be apparent

PREFACE

IN the intimate revelation of his own personality given in his book *Conflict and Dream* Dr. Rivers referred to his investigations in social organization as " the scientific problem which forms perhaps my most important contribution to ethnology " (p. 133) ; and he has made it clear in the same book that the claims of ethnology were so insistent as to have decided him to abandon work in physiology, medicine, and psychology, in each of which branches of science he had achieved conspicuous success, both in original research and teaching, in order to devote his whole attention to the urgent problems of the study of man. On his own admission his work on Social Organization was his greatest achievement in his chosen field of investigation. Hence it became my primary object as his literary executor to rescue everything that he had written on the subject.

This book is based upon the manuscript prepared by Dr. Rivers in 1920 and used by him in two courses of lectures in Cambridge in 1921 and 1922. It had been his intention to revise his manuscript in the summer of 1922 for a course of lectures in India during the winter 1922–3, and to publish it in the form of a book. While recognizing the imperative duty of getting the manuscript published, I realized that it consisted of little more than lecture notes, which needed drastic editing, such as Rivers himself proposed to bestow upon them, before they could be published. It was a great relief to me when Mr. Perry undertook the difficult and onerous task of preparing this work for the Press, for no one else has either the special knowledge of the evidence or the sympathetic understanding of Rivers' attitude towards the problems discussed in the book.

In the original manuscript there was a lack of coherence and consistency in the various chapters, especially in those dealing with kinship and marriage ; and the ambiguities had to be cleared up. In certain cases where the meaning of the author was not quite clear Mr. Perry substituted for doubtful passages quotations from Rivers' earlier writings, more especially *The History of Melanesian Society* and *Kinship and Social Organization*, and thus made certain that his real opinion was given to the reader. In the course of this adjustment Chapters II, III, and IV had to be in large measure rewritten, and Mr. Perry has added an Appendix (III) to make clear his own attitude with regard to what is known as the " Dual Organization ". I urged this course on him because during the session when Dr. Rivers was delivering these lectures in Cambridge for the last time Mr. Perry was writing his book on *The Children of the Sun*, which deals with some of the problems discussed in this book, but from a different angle. When I saw Dr. Rivers a fortnight before his death he told me that he was looking forward to the summer vacation (of 1922), when he intended to read the manuscript of Perry's book, and by discussion with him hoped to clear away the discrepancies in their interpretations of the evidence relating to social organization, and especially the question of the dual organization. It is a great misfortune that his death should have occurred before this colloquium could take place.

In urging Mr. Perry to deal in this drastic fashion with parts of the book I was prompted by the desire not only to make the book as coherent and lucid a guide as possible for the students, who will make it their vade-mecum, but also to do what Dr. Rivers himself would have done had he been spared to prepare the book himself. Although the chapters mentioned have been recast, the rest of the book is essentially as it was when Rivers died, except for a few minor literary corrections.

Realizing that the book is certain to be the standard text-book upon a very difficult subject and an enduring memorial of the author, who inaugurated the great advance in ethnological technique expressed in it, Mr. Perry has devoted a vast amount of time and labour to the preparation of the manuscript for the Press. In fact, he has done so much that his name ought to appear as part-author; but he has preferred to give lucid expression and consistency to Dr. Rivers' views rather than obtrude his own opinions.

A work which deals with the foundations of society cannot be stripped of all its puzzling intricacies; but in this book the problems have been put into the simplest possible form of expression. It might, perhaps, help in understanding the exposition if at the outset the reader studies the first and third Appendices and examines the concrete illustration of the principles of social organization which in Appendix III Mr. Perry has quoted from the Old Testament. Mr. Perry is responsible for all the bibliographical references (excepting those in Appendix I) as well as for the note on Bibliography which follows the Preface.

For permission to reprint, as Appendix I in this book, the illuminating article written in 1907 by Dr. Rivers " On the Origin of the Classificatory System of Relationships ", which was published in the *Anthropological Essays presented to E. B. Tylor*, I wish to express my gratitude to the Secretary of the Clarendon Press in Oxford.

G. ELLIOT SMITH.

UNIVERSITY COLLEGE,
LONDON.

BIBLIOGRAPHY

ALTHOUGH the literature of ethnology in general is enormous, especially as regards descriptions of various peoples, there is but little yet written on the topics treated of in this book. It is certain that Rivers will stand alongside of Morgan and McLennan (see Appendix I) as one of the great pioneers in the study of social organization, but his work is of a far more scientific nature than that of his two predecessors, and his general results can hardly now be overturned. The reader should proceed to read Rivers' *Kinship and Social Organization*, and then go on to *The History of Melanesian Society* for a detailed investigation into the problems of social structure that have engaged his attention in this book. Books such as those by Westermarck, Lowie, Webster, and Frazer will give him ample references to authorities.

Bachofen, J. J., *Das Mutterrecht*, Stuttgart, 1861.
Brown, A. R., Three Tribes of Western Australia (*Journ. Roy. Anth. Inst.*, 1913).
Cunow, H., *Zur Urgeschichte der Ehe und Familie*, Stuttgart, 1912.
Frazer, Sir J. G., *Totemism and Exogamy*, 1910.
Hobhouse, L. T., *Morals in Evolution*, 1915.
Kohler, J., *Urgeschichte der Ehe*, Stuttgart, 1897.
Lowie, R. H., *Primitive Society*, New York and London, 1920.
Maine, Sir H., *Ancient Law*, 1861.
Morgan, L. H., Systems of Consanguinity and Affinity of the Human Family (*Smithsonian Contributions to Knowledge*, 17), 1871.

Morgan L. H., *Ancient Society*, New York, 1877.

McLennan, J. F., *The Patriarchal Theory*, London, 1885.

—— *Studies in Ancient History*, 1886.

—— *Studies in Ancient History*, Second Series, 1896.

Rivers, W. H. R., Origin of the Classificatory System of Relationship (*Anthropological Essays presented to E. B. Tylor*), Oxford, 1907.

—— *Kinship and Social Organization*, 1914.

—— *The History of Melanesian Society*, 1914.

—— Article "Marriage" in Hastings' *Encyclopædia of Religion and Ethics*, 1915.

—— Article "Mother-right", ibid.

Schurz, *Altersklassen und Männerbunde*, Berlin, 1902.

Webster, *Primitive Secret Societies*, New York, 1908.

Westermarck, E., *History of Human Marriage*.

W. J. P.

CONTENTS

CHAPTER I

SOCIAL GROUPINGS

THE FAMILY

SOCIAL ORGANIZATION

CHAPTER I

SOCIAL GROUPINGS

The Family

I SHOULD like to begin the consideration of my subject by a brief account of the place which I believe social organization occupies in the study of human culture. I am one of those who believe that the ultimate aim of all studies of mankind, whether historical or scientific, is to reach explanation in terms of psychology, in terms of the ideas, beliefs, sentiments, and instinctive tendencies by which the conduct of man, both individual and collective, is determined. This conduct, whether individual or collective, but particularly the collective, is also determined by the social structure of which every person who comes into the world finds himself a member. The object of this book is to give a general account of this social structure, of the social setting within which every human being, whether he forms an element in a great empire like ourselves, or is only a member of some rude savage tribe, has to feel, think, and act. It is possible to study the social setting in itself, quite apart from any psychological considerations, and that is the object, or should be the object, of what I like to call " pure sociology ", as distinguished from social psychology ; that is the general standpoint from which the subject is approached in the following chapters.

This social structure can be studied from two points of view. It may be our aim merely to describe the various forms of social structure found throughout the world, to analyse each into its constituent elements, to study the relation of these elements to one another, to inquire into the social functions of their constituent elements, and to discover how these functions are combined so that they succeed in producing an orderly and consistent organization.

The other point of view is the historical. It may be our aim to discover the processes by which human societies with their vast variety have come into being. During recent years students of human culture, and especially its more lowly forms, have been taking a great interest in this historical point of view, and, in their zeal towards this end, have perhaps neglected the task, which must always come first, of understanding human societies as they are, before they can expect to understand how they have come to be what they are. I propose, therefore, in this book to deal mainly with what may be called the static study of social organization, rather than with the more dynamic aspect which is so prominent in books on social and political institutions ; but I shall not neglect the. historical aspect, and shall try to describe, as well as I can, the present state of the chief controversies about the history of marriage, of the family, and of other social institutions.

The primary aim of this book will be the study of social organization as a process by which individuals are associated in groups. Instead of speaking of this subject as social organization, it would be equally appropriate to call it the study of social grouping, and of the division of social function which accompanies the grouping. The members of human societies, and I shall only deal with human societies, in spite of the temptation to consider the social grouping and accompanying functions of other forms of animal society, are grouped together in a large number of different ways ; and it will be one of my tasks to distinguish between, describe, define, and classify these various forms of grouping. As already indicated, I shall have to consider, not only the structure of the groups, but also their functions ; and the classification adopted will depend in the main upon the nature of these functions. These may be divided into two main groups : those concerned with the relation to one another of the individuals who form the group, and those concerned with the relations of the different groups to one another. (An important section of the second class will consist of relations between groups of similar function, but belonging to different communities or societies.)

The various functions appertaining to social groups are usually known as customs. Certain customs, or groups of customs, are so important, and take so fundamental a place in social organization, that they have been separated from other customs and called *Institutions*, a term not altogether happy, since it might be held to imply that they have been instituted by some kind of authority, or as the result of some kind of social contract, and have not developed. Consequently I am liable to have a sense of discomfort when I use the term, but it is so convenient as a means of designating such customs as marriage, property, chieftainship, and caste that I shall use it, only reminding the reader that the use of the term "institution" must not be held to imply that the customs so called have been instituted by any kind of authority or social contract.

It will be my frequent business in this book to consider the social organization of peoples of rude culture, of those we usually call savages. I shall not follow the example of many ethnological students of human society, and forget that there is a place called Europe, and even an island called Great Britain ; but, nevertheless, I shall deal very largely with societies widely different from our own, and I may perhaps devote some space to stating what I hold to be the special importance of savage societies in the study of social organization.

A leading character of these societies is the small number of social groups which it is possible to distinguish in them. This is partly due to the relatively great simplicity of the functions which these lowly societies have to perform ; but it is due in still larger measure—and it is this which gives them much of their theoretical interest —that these societies exhibit the working of the principle of division of social labour, or

differentiation of social function, in a very slight degree compared with such civilized societies as those of Europe and
Asia. Social functions which, among ourselves, are distributed
among many different social groups, may fall, in a lowly society,
to the lot of only one social group.   One result of this
performance of various social functions by one social group
is that it brings out clearly and obviously an interdependence
of the different kinds of social function which, though it
exists, tends to be concealed by the elaboration of our own
social system, so that this interdependence only becomes
obvious as the result of some social upheaval such as that with
which the world is confronted at the present moment. A feature
of social organization which, though well recognized by
historians or students or political science, only shows itself
clearly in our own case on special occasions to the ordinary
observer, is a striking and obvious character of the rude
societies which will form the chief subject-matter of this book.

Another aspect of these rude forms of social grouping which
is of theoretical interest is that they reveal clearly and obviously
a feature of social organization which, in spite of its
fundamental character, is so unobtrusive among ourselves
that it has been possible for an able and acute student, I refer
to Mr. G. D. H. Cole,[1] to speak of the institution of the family
as almost bereft of social functions. He clearly recognizes,
however, that the social groups which correspond to the family
in more primitive societies are social groups in the fullest
sense. I may say at once that, according to the view I shall
put forward, the social function of the family is to assign to
each individual born into a society the special place which he
or she is to occupy in that society.

As I have said, one of the chief tasks of this book will be to
demonstrate the low degree of differentiation of social function
which is characteristic of the ruder forms of social organization.
If we were to limit our attention to these ruder societies,
however, it would be difficult, if not impossible, to recognize

[1] *Social Theory*, p. 12, London, 1920.

distinctions of social function with sufficient definiteness to allow us to use them as the basis of a classification. In order to place this classification on a satisfactory foundation it will be convenient to turn to our own society, and to consider briefly the chief varieties of social grouping which it reveals.

First, there is that form of social grouping, of which the family is the most striking example among ourselves, which, as I have already indicated, not only determines to a large extent the social position which each child is to occupy in the social order, but also determines all those intimate, though through their familiarity unobtrusive, relations which are connected with the concept of " home ". It is a striking example of the unobtrusive nature of this form of social grouping that students of human society have not found it necessary to use any special term for this kind of social grouping, which I propose to term *Domestic*.

The second form of social grouping to be mentioned is the *Political*. In our own society, with its high degree of differentiation of social function, there are many varieties of this form of grouping. Thus, each one of us is a member of an empire, a nation, a county, a parish, and the life of each is regulated by the actions of a parliament, a cabinet, government departments, municipal corporations, or county, urban, or parish councils, together with many other bodies that regulate special departments of social activity. The social functions performed among ourselves by this great variety of social grouping may, in a simple community, fall to the lot of only two or three social groups ; and even these groups often exist in so unorganized a form that it may be difficult to recognize their existence, and to realize that they perform functions for which our more elaborate needs have produced so complex a machinery.

The third class of social groupings to be mentioned are those concerned with the economic aspect of social life. I shall speak of these as *Occupational Groupings*. Here, as in the case of the political grouping, the division of social labour in rude societies has taken place to so slight an extent that, in some of the societies we shall consider, it will be difficult to recognize whether this form of social grouping exists at all.

The next kind of grouping is concerned with *Religion*. I may say here that if I were arranging forms of grouping in the order of relative importance which they occupy among the ruder forms of human society, I should be inclined to put religious grouping in the second instead of the fourth place. Variety and specialization of religious function are distinctly more obvious than variety and specialization of secular occupation.

A fifth mode of grouping is that concerned with *Education*. This with its great variety among ourselves of university, college, school groupings, etc., is also of a far more simple kind in lowly societies, where we find no form of social group entirely devoted to the purpose of education.

A sixth group is made up of the *Societies* or *Clubs* in which individuals associate together for some common purpose, often, among ourselves, connected with some form of play-activity, or for the closely related pursuits of art or science. A form of association which is of especial importance in rude societies is that in which knowledge of the purpose and main proceedings of the association is withheld from the rest of the community, the so-called *Secret Societies*. These associations, which take a relatively unimportant place in the social life of our own community, bulk very largely in some rude societies, and have social functions of so important a kind that it will be necessary to consider them at some length in a later chapter.

The development of associations in connexion with industry, such as guilds, trade unions, and federations of employers on the side of production, and co-operative societies on the side of production and consumption, now form important links in all civilized societies between groupings of the sixth category and those of the economic kind, and associations for educational purposes form similar links with the educational forms of grouping ; and we should try to discover traces of groups with corresponding functions in lowly societies.

All these different kinds of grouping are characterized by the feature of *Organization*. Membership of the group, and the process of joining and leaving the group, are the subject of definite social regulations, and involve certain duties and privileges in relation to the other members of the group. In order to illustrate this feature of organization, I may give an instance of a relation which should not be included as a form of social grouping as I use the expression here. All the people who on a given day read *The Times* or *The Daily Herald* might be regarded as a social group. These persons might be regarded as forming a social group, inasmuch as they all use the same means of gaining information about social and political events, and tend to have their opinions moulded in a similar manner ; but I do not include this relation among social groups, because it has no fixity, and is wholly unorganized. The people who read *The Times* vary from day to day, and the readers have no duties or privileges in relation to one another. If, on the other hand, a number of persons, even as few as two or three, associate themselves together to purchase and use *The Times* or *The Daily Herald* in common, we should have a characteristic example of a social group in the sense in which I use the term, though one of a very simple kind.

Before I pass on to deal with different modes of social grouping, I should like to mention one character which serves to distinguish some from others. The grouping I have just mentioned is a good example of a *Voluntary Association*, into which its members enter with full knowledge of what they are doing, and of the aims which the association is designed to fulfil. At the other end of the scale we have such an institution as the family, of which an individual person becomes a member without any act of volition, and by means of social regulations and traditions over which he has no control of any kind. We shall see later that, in many societies, membership of the

family may depend on a definite process of adoption ; and this
process is, of course, not unknown among ourselves. But, as
a rule, membership of the family, and still more constantly
membership of the social group of lowly societies, lies purely
outside individual or social volition, and is immediately
determined by the nature of the social organization. In this
distinction between different kinds of social grouping there
are many points of similarity between the voluntary and
involuntary activities of the individual. As in the case of
individual activity, there are many intermediate gradations
between the two. In a classification on these lines the domestic,
political, and religious groupings would, on the whole, fall
under the involuntary mode of grouping ; while secret societies,
co-operative societies, societies for the pursuit of art, science,
or play, and clubs generally would fall under the voluntary
variety of grouping. In our own society occupational grouping
would, in general, fall into the voluntary class, but in many
of the societies this grouping is of the involuntary kind.

Having thus tried to make clear what I mean by a social
group, I propose now to proceed to a brief survey of some of
the chief forms of social grouping of the involuntary kind, viz.
the different forms of the family, the clan or sib, the moiety of
the dual organization, and the tribe. Before I begin this survey
it may be well to point out how very defective is our knowledge
of these modes of grouping, and to mention why this should
be so.

Most of our knowledge of rude societies is derived from
persons who have travelled or dwelt among savage or barbarous
peoples, and have recorded what they have observed, but have
employed no special methods of inquiry, and have had no
special knowledge of sociological theory. It has been easy for
them to observe the nature of the material culture in general,
the character, for instance, of houses, clothing, weapons,
utensils, and such obvious practices as tattooing, distension
of the ear-lobe, circumcision, etc. When, as is frequently the
case, the observers have been missionaries, it is natural that

they should have recorded, as far as possible, the nature of the religious rites and beliefs, and almost universally the tales told by lowly peoples are a favourite subject for record and inquiry. It is only exceptionally, however, that we are given more than the scantiest record of social organization, and usually such records as are made have neither the exactness nor the detail which the student of social organization needs. One of the chief reasons for this is that social organization, fundamental as it is, and just because of this fundamental character, is unobtrusive. It does not force itself upon the attention of the observer from elsewhere. Its details only become apparent as the result of definite inquiry, while exact knowledge is hardly possible without the use of special methods. A characteristic example of this difficulty is presented by the topic of kinship, with which I shall deal in the fourth chapter. Thus, to take an example from one country only, there is little doubt that vast numbers of Europeans who spend their working lives in India come away at the end without having learnt that many of the peoples of that country have a system of relationship so widely different from our own, that no English term of relationship can be used in describing Indian society without serious danger of misunderstanding ; while, in spite of many records given to us by such authorities as Crooke,[1] Risley,[2] Thurston,[3] and Russell,[4] we still have to be content with vague knowledge, in place of the exact and detailed information which we owe to precise and systematic inquiry on Australia, Oceania, North America, and several parts of Africa.

Another source of vagueness and uncertainty is the unsatisfactory nature of sociological terminology, and the fact that such terms as family, clan, descent are not used in any

[1] W. Crooke, *The Tribes and Castes of the North-Western Provinces and Oudh*, Calcutta, 1896.

[2] Sir H. Risley, *Tribes and Castes of Bengal*, Calcutta, 1891.

[3] E. Thurston, *Tribes and Castes in Southern India*, Madras, 1909.

[4] R. V. Russell, *The Tribes and Castes of the Central Provinces of India*, 1916.

well-defined sense. The necessity for such definition is so imperative if we are to understand social organization, that I shall make no excuse for devoting much space to attempts at such definition.

The Family.— In the survey upon which I can now enter I will begin with the various kinds of social group which are included under the general heading of the family.

This term is used in the English language and in relation to our own culture in two senses, which must be carefully distinguished from one another if the word is to have any scientific value. When we speak of family life, and refer to the family as the basis of our society, we mean by the family a small social group consisting of parents and children ; but when I speak of a more or less distant relative as belonging to my family, or when we speak of the great ruling families of England, we are using the term in a very different and much more extended sense. When I use the term " family " without qualification I shall take it to have the first of these two senses : I shall use it to denote the simple social group consisting of parents and children. The exact form of the family will depend upon the nature of marriage. With monogamy the only complication arises where a person has married more than once, and has children by each marriage. A characteristic case is that in which a widower and widow, each with children, marry and have offspring. It will be most convenient to regard such a case as a combination of three families. A similar complication arises in the case of polygyny. In that variety of this practice where each wife has her own establishment, it will be most convenient to hold that there are a number of families with a common factor, the father and husband ; but where all the wives live together, and children are not distinguished according to their mothers, the case is more difficult, and it will be most convenient to speak of a polygynous family. The similar complication arising out of polyandry may be treated in the same manner, and we may speak of the polyandrous family. In all these cases the family

group is a simple one, involving only the relationships of
parent and child, brother and sister, using those terms in their
customary English senses.

If now we turn to the group of a wider kind, for which the
term " family " is also employed in ordinary speech, we meet
with a more difficult and complicated problem. The first point
to note is whether the group to be considered is " bilateral "
or " unilateral ".[1] By this I mean whether those included
in the group comprise relatives through the father only or
through the mother only, a form of grouping termed unilateral,
or through both father and mother, a form of grouping termed
bilateral.

It is necessary to distinguish between these two varieties
because they are confused together in the ordinary use of the
term in the English language. Thus, when we speak of one of
the great English political families, such as the Cecils or the
Cavendishes, we are using the term in the unilateral sense,
and are referring to a grouping determined by relationship
through the father. When, on the other hand, I speak of a
person as belonging to my family, though in the majority of
cases I should be taken to refer to one of my own name, and
therefore to a group unilaterally determined by relationship
through the father, this is not certain. In scientific usage it is
very important to distinguish between the bilateral and
unilateral modes of determination of the scope of the term.

The best modern example with which I am acquainted of the
bilateral variety is from Eddystone Island, in the western
part of the Solomon Islands. Here the most important social
group is one called *taviti*. This group consists of all those
persons with whom genealogical relationship other than by
marriage can be traced, whether through the father or the
mother. Since pedigrees are preserved for about four
generations, this means that a person includes in the group
he calls *taviti* all those whom we should call first, second, or

---

[1] See also Lowie. *Primitive Society*, chap. iv.

third cousins, whether related through the father or the
mother.   So far as we know, this bilateral variety of this
form of grouping is rare, and the unilateral determination of
the scope of the grouping is more frequent.   But we are in
need of more exact information on this point than is usually
provided by recorders of social organization.   In the past
there is definite evidence of the bilateral grouping in northern
Europe.[1] Except in a few places, of which our own country
appears to have been one, definite social functions, such as
payment of wergeld, fell to groups of kinsmen on both the
father's and the mother's side, no distinction being made
between them.

Let us pass now to the groups usually included under the
heading of the family, membership of which is counted
unilaterally, i.e. by relationship either through the father
alone, or through the mother alone.   These two modes of
determining membership of the group would naturally
produce two main varieties of the unilateral grouping.   The
so-called patriarchal family, which has played, and still plays,
so large a part in the speculations of social theorists, would be
an example of one variety, while the so-called matriarchal
family would be an example of the other.

The most definite example at present known of a mode of
social grouping which would fall under the first head, is the
joint or undivided family prevalent over the greater part of
India. This form of social grouping consists of persons related
in the male line, a characteristic group of the kind consisting
of a man, his sons, and his son's sons. Similar groups almost
certainly exist elsewhere, and there seems to be little doubt
that they were characteristic of certain societies of Northern
Europe, such as those of Ditmarschen, Norway, and our own
country, thus differing from other parts of Northern Europe,
where, as I have already said, the corresponding group, i.e.
group of corresponding functions, was of the bilateral kind,

[1] See B. S. Philpotts, *Kindred and Clan*, Cambridge, 1913.

and was determined by relationship through both father and mother.

In some respects this unilateral form of grouping resembles that usually known as the clan, which I shall consider shortly. As we shall see, the clan is pre-eminently a unilateral form of social grouping, and differs fundamentally from the bilateral grouping of the Solomons or of Northern Europe. The resemblance to the clan is perhaps even more striking in that variety of the family, in the extended sense, in which membership is determined by relationship through the mother. Here, again, our most characteristic example comes from India. In his standard book on *Hindu Law and Custom* J. D. Mayne speaks of the *taravad* of the Nayars of Malabar as the most perfect example of the joint family which exists in India.[1] The *taravad* of the Nayars consists of a group of persons who trace their relationship to one another in a definite way. A characteristic group of this kind will consist of a man, his sisters, the children of these sisters, and the children of their daughters, but not the children of their sons. It is a group of exactly the same kind as the joint family of other parts of India, except that its membership is determined by relationship through the mother, instead of by relationship through the father.

It is thus clear that, in ordinary language, and largely also in works supposed to be of a scientific kind, the term " family " is used to denote four different kinds of group : (i) the small group of parents and children ; (ii) the bilateral group, consisting of persons related through both father and mother ; (iii) the unilateral group of persons related through the father only ; and (iv) a fourth group, of a unilateral kind, consisting of persons related through the mother only. It is essential to distinguish these four forms of grouping, and it will naturally be convenient also to distinguish them in nomenclature.

As I have already said, I propose to confine my use of the term family, when used without qualification, to the group

[1] J. D. Mayne, *A Treatise on Hindu Law and Custom*, Madras, 1914.

consisting of parents and children. The other forms of grouping, for which terms are needed, are sometimes spoken of as examples of the extended family or the great family, corresponding with the German term " Grossfamilie ".

This nomenclature fails to distinguish between the bilateral and unilateral forms, a distinction which is of the greatest importance. For the bilateral group, I propose to use the term *Kindred*. When I speak of a kindred, I shall mean a group consisting of persons related to one another, other than by marriage, through both father and mother.

For the unilateral groups I believe it will be most convenient to adopt the terms in use in works on Indian law and sociology, and to speak of the *Joint Family*, distinguishing the two main varieties of the joint family as patrilineal and matrilineal respectively.

Before I pass on to the next main mode of social grouping, I must mention a group which, while corresponding in many respects with the family, simple or joint, yet differs from it. I refer to the *Household*. Among ourselves the social group formed by the household often differs from the family. It often includes members of the kindred as well as of the family proper, while sons will set up their own household and no longer form part of the household of the parents, and daughters will separate to form part of the households of their husbands. On the other hand, the household often includes, whether as servants or in some other capacity, persons who do not belong to the family at all, in any sense in which the term is used.

The members of the joint family of India often live together, and form a joint household corresponding in extent to the joint family, but the household often includes a sister's son or a daughter's son, who do not strictly speaking belong to joint family, though through the fact of common habitation they are often regarded as forming part of it.

I do not know of any example in which the group I call a kindred live together in one household, at any rate, as a systematic institution, though probably occasional cases occur.

CHAPTER II

SOCIAL GROUPINGS

CLAN, MOIETY, AND TRIBE

CHAPTER II

SOCIAL GROUPINGS

CLAN, MOIETY, AND TRIBE

THIS chapter will be devoted to the further examination of involuntary associations, those social groups into which a child is born, and of which it automatically becomes a member. One of the chief objects of the last chapter was to make clear the nature of the concept of " family ". We found that, not only as used in ordinary language, but also in works on anthropology or political science, the term denotes social groups of at least four different kinds. Our next business will be to consider the social group usually known as the *clan*. As we shall find, this customary term is not altogether suitable, and an alternative word will be suggested, but for the present the former will be used.

A committee which considered the matter a few years ago put forward as the definition of a clan that it is " An exogamous division of a tribe the members of which are held to be related to one another by some common tie, it may be belief in descent from a common ancestor, common possession of a totem, or habitation of a common territory ".[1]

One prominent feature of the clan which might be added to the definition is that it is a characteristic example of a unilateral mode of grouping, so that a person belongs to the clan of his father or to the clan of his mother ; and his fellow-clansmen are primarily related to him either through his father or through his mother, though intermarriage may lead to relationship to the clans of both parents.

As the clan is a unilateral grouping, it is evident that it resembles the two kinds of joint-family more closely than what

---

[1] See *Anthropological Notes and Queries*, London ; also *The Hand-Book of Folk-Lore*, p. 295, London, 1913.

I have called the kindred ; and, as a matter of fact, the resemblance is very close.   Thus, I had always regarded the *taravad*, the matrilineal [1] joint-family of the Nayars of Malabar as a clan.   The chief English account of this group describes it as exogamous, for instance, and it was only as the result of discussions with a Nayar member of my class that I came to the conclusion that it probably should be regarded as an example of a joint-family rather than a clan.   It may help to understand the matter if their points of resemblance and difference are considered.

The essential difference between the two is that the members of a joint-family can trace their relationships to one another, and express them genealogically, while this cannot necessarily be done by members of a clan.   If you ask a member of a joint family to state the nature of his relationship to another member, he can always describe it in terms of kinship, and can express it by means of a genealogical table.   A member of a clan can also do this with regard to many members of his group, but he cannot do so in other cases ; he can only express the relationship in one or other of the three ways stated in the definition of a clan (see p. 19).

To turn now to the matter of terminology, to which reference has already been made.   The term " clan " which has been used is that generally employed by British writers, and it has been adopted also by French sociologists.   The use of the term, derived from the social group of Scotland, which corresponds much more nearly with the tribe, has certain disadvantages. Many attempts have been made to introduce a different term. Thus the late Andrew Lang and Sir James Frazer have proposed to use the word " kin ".   They speak, for instance, of the totem-kin instead of the totemic clan.   Similarly, American ethnologists have used the word " gens ", which, in its original meaning, was a characteristic example of this form of social grouping ; but this term has only been used by them to denote the patrilineal variety of the group, and they have continued

[1] See p. 86 for the meaning of the word "matrilineal".

to use the word " clan " for the corresponding group, in which membership depends on relationship through the mother. I-tried to persuade the Committee already mentioned to adopt the less familiar word *sept* in place of clan. The Irish sept was probably not exogamous, but the word is so much less familiar than " clan " that there would not be the same likelihood of confusion.

In his book on *Primitive Society* [1] Lowie has adopted the allied word " sib ", and speaks of the sib wherever we are accustomed to speak of the clan. When I proposed the use of the word " sept " as an alternative for clan, I also suggested that " sib " should be used as a term for the relationship set up by membership of the sept. If it were adopted, the word " sib " would bear the same relation to the sept that the word " kin " bears to the family in its different forms. Thus, as members of the family, either in its pure or in its unilateral or bilateral forms, may be said to be " kin " to one another, so members of the sept would be " sib " to one another. This form of nomenclature would be very convenient if it were adopted ; but for the purpose of this book the customary word " clan " will be retained, and the word " sibship " will denote clan-relationship. It may be noted, in passing, however, that both " sept " and " sib " are related to the word " Sippe ", which is the customary German word for the clan.

Totemism

One of the most frequent, almost certainly the most frequent, form of the clan is one in which all its members believe in their relationship to a species of objects, animal, plant, or inanimate, called totems, of which animal totems are by far the most frequent. The exact nature of the relationship to the animal or other totem varies in different parts of the world. In some places, as in Melanesia, there is a definite belief that all the members of the totemic clan are descended from the totem. In other cases, also frequent in Melanesia, it is believed that

[1] p. 111.

the members of the clan are descended from a man or woman, who was in some way connected with the animal, plant, or inanimate object, which forms the totem of the group. In these cases, it is a question whether the real tie between the members of the clan is not belief in common descent in some form or another, whether this descent be from an animal, plant, or inanimate object or from a human ancestor. The totemic tie passes over by insensible gradations into the belief that the bond of union is descent from a common ancestor. If this be so, the relation called sibship (see p. 21) only differs from kinship in that the relationship is not capable of being traced genealogically.

The third kind of tie between the members of a clan mentioned in the definition is habitation of a common territory. In some forms of totemic organization the totemic tie covers the territorial tie, the group bound together by possession of a common totem occupying the same village or district. In the great majority of cases of totemism, however, this is not the case ; for several totemic groups occupy a village or district in common, and are mingled with one another, so that there is no local distinction between them. There are, however, many forms of clan organization in which the totemic bond is completely absent, where the essential tie between the members seems to be habitation of a common territory, without any evidence whatever of a totemic bond. In this case all the people of a village or district, or part of a village or district, believe themselves to be related to one another, and thus form a characteristic example of sibship. It has been suggested that all totemic clans were originally localized, and that the territorial clan is only a localized totemic group which has lost its totems. But this view is unsupported by evidence, and at present we must be content to accept the territorial tie as one form of bond between the members of a clan.

It is probable, however, that the territorial bond is another expression of the belief in common descent ; that the people of a village or district form a clan because they are descended from a common ancestor. One fact pointing in this direction is that, in cases which have come under my observation, membership of the clan does not depend on the actual habitation, but on the place to which a person or his ancestors originally belonged. It is probable that in all territorial clans the real bond is belief in common descent rather than habitation of a common territory.

Like the varieties of the joint-family, clans differ in counting relationship through the father or through the mother. This matter will be gone into in the chapter on mother-right and father-right. These varieties are distinguished as " gens " and " clan " by the American ethnologists.

It may be worth while asking whether there is any correlation between the mode of descent and the nature of the bond uniting the members of a clan. If the tie connecting the members of a totemic clan is the claim to descent from some one person, we should expect a difference in the relation to local grouping according as descent is patrilineal or matrilineal. For, if descent is patrilineal, and women taken as wives go to live with their husbands, we should expect the local grouping to correspond with the totemic clan ; whereas if children are brought up in the house of their mothers, while, for a time at any rate, they continue to take the totems of their fathers, there would soon cease to be any relation between local grouping and the totemic clans, which would be scattered about in different parts of the region occupied by the tribe. Unfortunately our information concerning the degree of local segregation of totemic clans is very defective, so that it is difficult to say whether there is that correspondence between the local grouping of totemic clans and patrilineal descent which should exist if the situation is as I have suggested. The island of Mabuiag in Torres Straits forms a good example of the association of a local grouping with patrilineal descent. In this island each clan formerly lived in one locality, and so clearly was this local character recognized that the people of a clan were often designated by the name of the place where the clan formerly lived. In most parts of Melanesia, on the other hand, the members of different clans live together indiscriminately, and this is certainly so where totemism is combined with matrilineal descent.

Another feature of totemism, to which I may now refer, is that the institution varies according to the nature of the totem. Three main varieties of totem can be recognized ; animals, plants and inanimate objects, such as stars, rain, or even manufactured objects. In many forms of totemism all three kinds of totem occur, animals being the most frequent ; but sometimes all, or the great majority of the totems are of some one kind, and this is especially so in connexion with certain classes of animal. The most definite example of this with which I am acquainted occurs in several parts of Melanesia, where all the totems of the community are birds, while else-where in Melanesia the majority of the totems are aquatic animals. There is also evidence that, in some places, all the exogamous clans of a community may be associated with plants.[1]

Sometimes a clan has more than one totem, as in British New Guinea. This is termed linked-totemism. In certain places, again, as in Australia, some animal is said to be connected with men, and another with women.

FUNCTIONS OF THE CLAN AND FAMILY

Having now examined the nature and varieties of the family and the clan, it is possible to consider their functions, dealing with them according to the classification laid down in the first chapter. Since the social functions of the family and clan are the more important, they will be left over till the next chapter ; only the political and other functions will be con-sidered here.

In the case of property the clan and the family both play a part. This produces a very complex system of ownership in places having the clan organization. For instance, as will be shown in the chapter on Property (Chapter VI), in the island of

---

[1] *History of Melanesian Society*, chap. xxx.

Ambrim in the New Hebrides property belongs both to the clan and to a group partaking of the nature of a kindred, consisting of near kin on the father's side and the sister's children of a man. Descent in Ambrim is through the father, and the clans are on a territorial basis. Uncultivated land is held to belong to the village or clan in common, but cultivated land belongs to the kindred group just mentioned, which is called the *vantimbül*. In Melanesia in general it is found that the property of such a group as that just mentioned is the common property of the group, every member having the absolute right to use any of the group property. But when a person not belonging to the group wishes to use it, he has to ask permission of one of the group owing the property, a right which is rarely, if ever, refused. This privilege of asking permission to use the property of a group seems often to belong to every member of the clan, and suggests the former existence of a much more diffused system of ownership than that which now obtains, possibly even a state in which property was common to the clan.

Thus it is evident from Melanesia that property is not vested in the family in the limited sense, or in the clan, but in some form of the joint family or kindred.

In North America, as in Melanesia, there are many inter-mediate stages between individual and common ownership; but, again, as in Melanesia, common ownership, when present, seems to be vested in some form of the joint family rather than in the clan or sib. The case which has been supposed to point most definitely to ownership by the clan is that of the Aztecs; but it is doubtful whether the groups supposed to be clans really had that nature. The balance of evidence seems to be against it, so that here also the state was probably one of ownership by a patrilineal joint-family.

We may regard property as a subject lying between the political and economic functions of social groups. The more purely economic subject of occupation will be dealt with later,[1]

[1] See Chapter VIII.

but it can be said here that, wherever we find specialized
hereditary occupations, these are associated either with the
individual family, or with special groups such as the caste.
There does not seem to be a case in which the clan has as its
function the following of a special occupation.

Another class of social function of the clan is that associated
with religion.   Here the chief topic of interest turns on the
religious aspects of totemism. In some cases the totem is purely
a sign or emblem devoid of any sanction which can be regarded
as religious, the prohibition on eating or killing the totem not
involving belief in the action of any higher power ; but in most
forms of totemism there seems to be a definite reverence for
the totem, especially when it is a species of animal. Injuring,
killing and eating the totem are believed to bring upon
the offender calamities dependent on the activity of a higher
power More rarely, as in Australia, the members of the totemic
clan are believed to have the power, by means of suitable
rites, to multiply the totemic species ; but it may be noted that
the belief in these powers is associated with a relatively small
importance of the totemic group as a form of social organization,
it having no definite place, for instance, in the regulation of
marriage. It would appear as if totemism is a form of social
grouping which, in its usual form, has both domestic and
religious functions, and that different kinds of totemism form
a series which passes from social functions, at one end of the
scale, to religious (or magical) functions, at the other end.

In the purely territorial form of the clan, I do not know of
any functions which can be regarded as religious, and this
perhaps may be held to confirm the view, suggested earlier,
that this form of grouping is one in which the relation to the
ancestor from whom the group is descended has become even
more unconscious than in the case of totemism.

It is often found that the clan, as a unit of the larger grouping
of the tribe, possesses certain rites which it performs on behalf
of the tribe. Thus, for example, in the Omaha tribe, a branch
of the Sioux family, the clan connected with the elk had rites

associated with war, and the other clans had their corresponding rites.[1]

The clan plays an important part in the political constitution of the community at large. For, throughout the world, each clan has its own council, composed of the older generation of males, which transacts all its business. The clan usually has the right to elect its own chiefs, when it has any, and depose them, without regard to the council of the larger unit of which it forms a part.

The function of the clan as a regulator of marriage will be considered later (see p. 39).

THE DUAL ORGANIZATION

It is found, especially in Melanesia, Australia, and North America, that many communities are divided into two distinct divisions, called *moieties*, which play a definite part in the life of the community, particularly in respect of the regulation of marriage.

The dual system of Melanesia is usually associated with matrilineal descent, a person belonging to his or her mother's moiety. Not long ago I should have said that the association with matrilineal descent was invariable, but Mr. Newsom has recently found that, in New Caledonia, there is a characteristic dual system with patrilineal descent.

One significant feature of the dual organization, in Melanesia and Australia, is that it appears to transcend the boundaries of tribes or island communities. Where the moieties have names it is found, in Melanesia, that these names agree in islands, which, so far as we know, have little in common as regards other features of social organization. This is also the case in Australia, where the moieties of many tribes, widely scattered over the continent, have similar names.

The dual system is combined with a local grouping, which seems to be the unit determining most social relations other

---

[1] Fletcher and la Flèsche, " The Omaha Tribe " : *27th Ann. Rep. (Bureau Amer. Eth.*, 1911).

than the regulation of marriage. Especially important is the strange feature that, though the chief purpose of the organization is the regulation that marriage shall always take place between members of the two moieties, these moieties are hostile to one another, and regard one another with dislike and suspicion, but I do not know of any cases of organized hostility between clans in Melanesia. In dual communities with matrilineal descent, a father and son will necessarily belong to different moieties, and will therefore be hostile to one another.

Closely connected with the hostility is the belief that the two moieties have different physical and mental characters. In several parts of Melanesia, for instance the Solomon Islands, it is believed, I do not know with how much foundation, that the members of the two moieties can be distinguished from one another by differences in physical character, and especially in the number and arrangement of the lines on the hands, and that they have different mental dispositions. One of the two moieties is usually regarded as superior to the other in social estimates.

A feature of interest, recently recorded by Dr. C. E. Fox in San Cristoval (in the Solomons), is that one of the two moieties of the central part of that island, viz. the moiety which is regarded as superior to the other, has a name which probably means stranger or sea-farer.

A dual division is frequent in North America, usually combined with other forms of social organization, the two primary groups being broken up into a number of sub-groups similar to the totemic clans of other parts of that continent. In some cases the grouping has little more than a ceremonial significance, or may even only show itself in games and mock contests. In a few cases, however, the dual grouping exists alone, for instance among the Haidahs of Queen Charlotte's Island, off British Columbia, where the whole community is broken up into two exogamous moieties with matrilineal descent. Another case occurs in California, where certain tribes, of which the most complete description comes from the Miwok, have two moieties comparable with those of Melanesia, and there is also the striking similarity with San Cristoval, that the two moieties are identified with land and water respectively. The Miwok differ, however, from the great majority of Melanesian instances of the dual system, in having patrilineal descent.

There is no evidence of hostility between the two moieties of the dual organization in America. Some kind of rivalry between them is common, and may be present when the dual character takes no part in the regulation of marriage, but it is purely ceremonial. Occasionally, however, one moiety is regarded as superior to the other, as in Melanesia.

We know of only one case [1] of an arrangement in Africa which can be classed with the dual organization. This is among the Gallas of East Africa, who are said by an early observer, Charles New, to be divided into two groups, called by him tribes or classes, the men of one tribe or class having to take their wives from the other.[2] Later writers on the Gallas have not mentioned this feature, though, as Frazer has pointed out, the statements of the most important (Paulitschke)[3] are so

---

[1] Graebner states that there are two other cases of dual organization, among the Ovambo (Schinz, *Deutsch-Südwest-Afrika*, 303 sqq. Rautanen in Steinmetz, *Rechtsverhältnisse von eingebornen Völkern in Afrika und Ozeanien*, 327 sqq.).

[2] " In regard to marriage they have a peculiar custom. They are divided into two tribes or classes, the Baretuma and the Harusi, and the men of each tribe have to select their wives from the other ; the Baretumas marry the Harusi and *vice versa*." Charles New, *Life, Wanderings, and Labours in Eastern Africa*, pp. 273 sqq., quoted in Sir J. G. Frazer, *Totemism and Exogamy*, ii, 541.

[3] Es ist erwähnt worden, dass die Oromo die Ehe unter nahen Verwandten zwar verabscheuen, dass er aber selbst zur Schwesterehe unter ihnen kommen könne. Die Wahl der Braut richtet sich nach dem Stande derselben, ob sie nämlich sich den Luba oder Birmadu—ein Art reinerer Gruppen von Oromo (wie die Borana) und ähnlich den Stammen und Classenunterscheiden der heutigen Juden—oder der Wata, d.i. den minder reinen oder vernehmen Gruppen der Oromo angehört. Luba und Wata heiratet nur unter einander. Zu diesen zwei Gruppen treten noch die Tumtu (Schmeide) und die Adagatta (Zauberer), deren Angehörwieder nur unter einander Ehen eingehen. Wata, Tumtu, und Adagatta stehen aber nur in einer Art Kastenverhältniss tiefer als die Luba. P. Paulitschke, *Ethnographie Nordost-Afrikas : Die materielle Cultur der Danakil, Galla und Somal*, p. 202, Berlin, 1893.

indefinite that the possibility of his having found a similar arrangement cannot be excluded. I do not know, however, of any other features of this dual system similar to those recorded so extensively in Melanesia and America.

In connexion with the distribution of the dual organization, it will be well to say one or two words about forms of social organization which resemble the dual system, and have frequently been confused with it. When a society consists of two classes, such as chiefs and commoners, it would be possible to speak of a dual organization, but unless they form an inter-marrying system, as in Melanesia and among the Gallas, there is no point in classing the two together. Cases intermediate between the two, however, occur. Thus, in the island of Vanua Lava in the Fijian Archipelago, there are two groups called *vosa*, and a man of one *vosa* must marry a woman of the other.[1] Moreover, the *vosa* is strictly matrilineal, although, as a general rule, Fiji is the seat of patrilineal institutions. The organization thus falls definitely into line with that of other parts of Melanesia, although Mr. Hocart was not able to discover any belief in differences in physical or mental characters.

The point to which attention is now called, is that one of the two *vosa* is called the *vosa turanga*, *turanga* being a customary Fijian term for chief or noble. Mr. Hocart expressly states that membership of this moiety has nothing to do with nobility, nobles and commoners being distributed through the two moieties ; but the use of this term may be significant, especially when taken together with the belief of the Banks Islands and San Cristoval, that the members of one moiety are superior to the others.

Though these facts suggest that there may have been in their past history some kind of relation between the dual intermarrying grouping and the division into chiefs and commoners, the two kinds of organization are so different that they should be kept apart in a classification of social groups.

[1] A. M. Hocart in *Man*, 1915, xv, 5.

Again, the Todas have two main groups, which, by several writers, including N. W. Thomas and R. H. Lowie, have been regarded as examples of the dual organization : but they resemble the organizations of Melanesia only in their duality, and otherwise have a wholly different character. Instead of marrying with one another the two Toda groups are strictly endogamous, and have relations with one another in which each resembles an Indian caste.[1] It is only dependence on a wholly superficial character which could lead to their system being classed with the dual system of Melanesia, of North America, or of the Gallas.

A more difficult case is that in which a dual exogamous system has come into existence through the dying out of all but two exogamous clans of a society which once possessed a larger number. In my book on *The Todas* I have described a state of affairs in one of the two sections of the tribe, in which the great growth of one clan and the disappearance of others is leading in this direction ; and it is possible that a dual intermarrying system which has been recorded among one section of the Gonds of Central India [2] may have arisen in some such way.

Another possible case of this kind is in the island of Ysabel, in the Solomons, where one district has only two moieties, while three is the number in other parts of the island, but in this instance the definite presence of the dual organization in other parts of the Solomons makes it possible that the dual character is original, and not the result of degeneration.

THE TRIBE

Although the food-gatherers wander about in family groups, peoples with moieties and clans are usually grouped together into larger units, called tribes. We are accustomed to speak of tribes only in connexion with relatively simple societies.

---

[1] [Rivers, *The Todas*. It must be remembered that Rivers is relying here on exogamy as the chief characteristic of the dual organization.]

[2] R. V. Russell, *The Tribes and Castes of the Central Provinces of India*, 1916, iii, 44, 63, 465.

The tribe shades off into groups of a more complex kind, such as the nation, and its exact definition is not easy. It may, however, be described as follows : " A tribe is a social group of a simple kind, the members of which speak a common dialect, have a single government, and act together for such common purposes as warfare." A negative character is that it is not exogamous, that is to say, there are no rules compelling its members to marry into other similar groups. On the other hand, it is usually more or less endogamous : its members usually marry within the group, but not rigorously enough to make it possible to use the practice as an essential feature of the definition.[1]

A feature often included in the definition of a tribe is its habitation of a common territory, but the nomadic habits of many groups, which in all general respects must be regarded as tribes, makes it difficult to include the geographical factor in the definition.[2]

One point must, however, be insisted on, namely, that the tribe is, in the main, a political rather than a domestic group, with a common speech as its main characteristic.

The tribe corresponds largely to the much debated variety of social grouping known as the nation. It is probable that students of political science would be greatly helped in their attempts to reach an understanding concerning what they mean by a nation if they were to take the far simpler tribe

---

[1] See p. 40 for a discussion of these terms.

[2] [It is probable that Rivers's definition needs correction. The exclusion of the territorial factor is probably erroneous, for even nomadic tribes have their habitual camping grounds. Again, the contention that a tribe has a single government and unites for common action does not accord with Professor A. R. Brown's statements with regard to certain tribes of West Australia. He states that they have no tribal chief and no form of tribal government ; also that the fights which formerly took place were not wars of one tribe against another, but of one part of one tribe against one part of another tribe, or, at times, of one part of one tribe against another part of the same tribe. Thus there was, he says, no unity of the tribe in warfare (A. R. Brown, *Journ. Roy. Anthr. Inst.*, 1913, p. 144).

It seems, on the whole, best to describe the tribe as a group speaking a common dialect and inhabiting a common territory.]

as their pattern, and regarded as a nation the social group which, in large communities, has social functions similar to those of the tribe. One of the chief processes by which the nation has evolved from the tribe is that of federation, and it is instructive that this process of federation of tribes into larger groups, approaching in character to the nations of the civilized world, may be followed in some places, as in North America. This process of federation, whether by peaceful or warlike means, enables us to understand, for instance, the great complexity introduced into the concept of "nation" as compared with "tribe" by the absence, or less definite presence, of a common language.

CLAN, MOIETY, AND TRIBE

[The proper understanding of the discussion of marriage and relationship which will begin in the next chapter is only possible when the relations between the clan, the moiety and the tribe are fully understood. The tribe is the larger unit which comprehends the other two, either singly or together. That is to say, a tribe may be divided into clans with no moieties; it may be divided into moieties with no clans of any sort, though this rarely, if ever, happens; and it may have both clans and moieties. From the historical point of view there seems to be no doubt that the earliest form of grouping is that of moieties and clans, each moiety being divided up into smaller groups. As has been said, the chief function of the moiety is the regulation of marriage: the clan fills governmental and other rôles in the life of the community, while, at the same time, playing its part, in some societies, in the regulation of marriage. The clan has its council, and certain members of each clan sit on the council of the tribe, or whatever the larger grouping may be. In this the clan differs profoundly from the moiety, which has no political functions whatever, so far as is known.]

CHAPTER III

MARRIAGE

CHAPTER III

MARRIAGE

I HAVE now dealt with the nature, and with certain functions, of different kinds of social groups. Incidentally I have mentioned the highly organized customs, or associations of customs, which we call institutions (see p. 5). I propose now to consider one of these institutions, one that, so far as domestic grouping is concerned, is the fundamental institution of human society, namely marriage.

I shall begin by considering the social functions of marriage. These are of two main kinds. Marriage can be considered as the means by which human society regulates the relations between the sexes. In the ordinary view of the institution this kind of social function takes the larger place, and undue emphasis has consequently been laid on this aspect of marriage, even in the scientific treatment of the subject, so that the close relation between this aspect of the subject and ethical considerations has definitely biased the comparative study of problems connected with marriage.

In this chapter I shall lay especial stress on the far more important function of marriage, as the means by which every individual born into a society is assigned a definite place in that society, by which his or her social relations to the rest of the society are determined. Each child, by virtue of being born as a child of a marriage, takes its place in the social structure. Certain members of the group are its relatives : others are not necessarily relatives, but they belong to the same clan or moiety ; certain members of the community of the opposite sex are possible mates, while others are forbidden : all these and other such relationships are determined by the act of birth into a family group. Looked at from this point of view, marriage may be an institution of the most definite and highly organized kind, although in its rôle as a regulator of sexual relations it may be of a very lax and imperfect order.

I shall begin by considering the means of regulating marriage. In every human society with which we have any extensive acquaintance, there are to be found definite rules regulating whom a person may or may not marry. These rules are of many different kinds, but they fall under two main heads :—

(i) Regulations in which genealogical relationship, or, as I shall term it, kinship, is concerned.

(ii) Regulations depending on membership of a social group such as a moiety or clan.

Marriage is practically always regulated by genealogical relationship, even when membership of a clan or moiety plays its part. Among European peoples, who have the family as their chief form of domestic grouping, persons are prohibited from marrying those to whom they are related in certain ways, the prohibitions being formulated by the " table of prohibited kindred and affinities ". But even among peoples with clans and moieties we find that kinship plays a great part in regulating marriage. Moreover, these regulations do not consist merely of prohibitions, as among us, but include rules enjoining certain   marriages   between   near   kin.   Thus   in   certain parts of India, in Australia, Melanesia, North America and elsewhere, it is, or has been, the common practice for a man to marry the daughter of his mother's brother or father's sister, that is to say, his cross-cousin, as she is called. It is even probable, as in Australia, that many peoples permitted only this form of marriage. In other forms of marriage between near kin that are practised systematically by certain peoples, a man may marry his brother's daughter, his brother's granddaughter, the wife of his mother's brother or his father's sister, his daughter's daughter, the daughter of his sister's son, the daughter of his mother's brother.   In all these cases the relative in question is the normal person to marry. These forms of marriage just mentioned will play an important part in the general discussion on kinship relations in connexion with the classificatory system of relationship (see p. 68).

Other forms of marriage between near kin are known. In one vast community, that of the followers of the Mohammedan religion, it is orthodox to marry cousins of all kinds, and preference is given to the marriage of a man with the daughter of his father's brother.

Another form of marriage of relatives which must be mentioned is that of brother and sister, and sometimes even of mother and son. This was, as is well known, a custom of certain royal families of antiquity, such as those of Egypt, Persia and Peru, and it still exists, or has existed in recent times, in the Hawaiian Islands, where it is also limited to the royal families, or, at least, to the class of chiefs. In these islands the highest kind of chief was one who was the child of brother and sister, who were themselves again the offspring of this kind of marriage.

There have been many theories as to the origin of this form of marriage. In the Hawaiian Islands this custom existed side by side with a repugnance among the commoners, not only to marriage with a sister, but with any person with whom blood relationship could be traced.

THE MOIETY AND CLAN AS REGULATORS OF MARRIAGE

These two social groups play an important part in regulating marriage. For it is usually found, among peoples with one or both of these social groups, that no one may marry a member of his or her moiety or clan. [In those cases where the moiety of the tribe is subdivided into a number of clans, the rule is that no one may marry a member of the same moiety, so that the clan does not function in that respect, marriage being forbidden, not only between members of the same clan, but also between members of clans that belong to the same moiety.] But where the community consists only of clans, the rule, where one exists at all, is that marriage must not take place within the clan.

It may happen that communities exist in which the moiety or clan exists as the only mechanism to regulate marriage, but no such case is known. It is always found that kinship plays some part, in that certain relatives are favoured or regular mates. The fundamental institution of the family thus plays its part in all forms of society.

Exogamy and Endogamy

In the discussion of the marriage regulations associated with moieties and clans two technical terms have come into general use, namely *Exogamy* and *Endogamy*. By exogamy is understood the regulation that a member of a social group must find a mate in another social group: by endogamy is meant the regulation whereby a mate must be found within the group.

These terms need some consideration, for they have been the source of some confusion. For instance, it has been thought that exogamy and endogamy were processes more or less opposed to one another. Even so critical a writer as Andrew Lang fell into this error, and supposed that a community could not be at once exogamous and endogamous. This misunderstanding is due to failure to appreciate the fact that the two terms apply properly to two different kinds of social group. Probably the confusion goes back to a misunderstanding on the part of McLennan, to whom we owe the term " exogamy ". Relying on certain imperfect records, McLennan supposed that the custom he called exogamy was one in which every member of the tribe is compelled to marry a member of another tribe, and he linked up the institution with the custom of marriage by capture. We now know that if this kind of exogamy, that is tribal exogamy, exists at all, it is very exceptional. As we now use the term, exogamy is a custom in which a person may not marry into his or her own moiety or clan (sib) or other constituent group of the tribe. The rule has nothing whatever, so far as is known, to do with the tribe itself, of which the moiety and clan are constituent groups.

Endogamy only really applies to the castes of India and similar groupings in other parts of the world. Since the caste contains a number of exogamous groups, it is seen that exogamy and endogamy can be two complementary modes of marriage regulation. Endogamy may apparently be a rule in the tribe, if, owing to geographical or social isolation, its members are unable to find mates elsewhere ; but usually there is no sentiment against marriages with members of other tribes, and marriages of this kind take place whenever opportunity arises. In such a case there is no point in speaking of the practice as endogamy, for it is not a more or less fixed rule forbidding members of the tribe to seek their mates elsewhere. As an institution endogamy therefore is much less widespread than exogamy.

[Exogamy connected with the clan must be distinguished from exogamy connected with the moiety. In the case of the moiety marriage must be into the other moiety of the community, or, often, into the moiety corresponding to it in other communities. In the case of the clan the rule depends upon whether the dual organization is present or not. If it is present, members of all clans in the same moiety are forbidden mates, and usually those of all other clans in the other moiety are possible mates. Where the dual grouping is not present, marriage is usually allowed with every other clan.] In some cases, where the dual grouping is absent, marriage is prohibited with certain clans other than a man's own, the choice of these clans being usually determined by kinship. A man, for instance, may be prohibited from marrying into the clans of his two parents or of his four grand-parents, this rule arising through the combination of exogamy and regulation by kinship.

It is evident that a close relationship exists between exogamy and the unilateral character which distinguishes the social groups concerned. If membership of the moiety or clan were not determined unilaterally, on the one hand, or if the rule of exogamy were not strictly kept, the whole system of the moiety or clan would be disorganized, and confusion would take the place of the definite and orderly grouping which results from the action of the two kinds of regulations.

Although the moiety and clan provide the most definite examples of exogamy, this practice is also followed by certain forms of the family.   The bilaterally determined group of Eddystone Island, the *taviti* (see p. 13), might be called exogamous. In this island the *taviti* of a person is a group made up of all the persons with whom he can trace genealogical relationship other than by marriage, and since he is prohibited from marrying any of these persons, the *taviti* group may be regarded as another example of an exogamous social group, but less strictly defined. Again, in China, where no persons possessing the same surname are allowed to marry, the group corresponding to our Smiths or Browns would be exogamous. We could perhaps regard the family proper, in the limited sense, as an exogamous group, though the fact that in this case the marriage is equally regulated by kinship makes it unnecessary to use this form of expression.

POLYGYNY AND POLYANDRY

We have so far dealt with forms of marriage arising out of regulations concerning the social status of the persons who enter into a union.   It is now necessary to consider the forms of marriage in which a number of persons enter into union.

The practice of a person being married to more than one partner is usually known as polygamy, but since the marriage of a man with several wives is so far more frequent and better known than other forms of multiple union, this word has come widely to denote this latter kind of marriage. To avoid possible confusion, the marriage of one man with several women will be termed *polygyny*, and if the term polygamy is used at all, it will be for multiple unions. The union of one woman with several husbands is *polyandry*, while the disputable form of marriage in which several husbands are married to several wives is usually known as *group-marriage*.

The most frequent of these forms of marriage is polygyny. It may exist in different forms, according as the wives live together or have different establishments, but it does not raise any specially interesting or difficult problems. The only point I need mention about it is that everywhere, so far as we know, it is not universal, but is the privilege of the powerful and rich.

The part of the world where the practice flourishes with the greatest luxuriance is Africa, where kings and chiefs may have even hundreds of wives, and it is here also that we find especially the feature that the wives have different establishments, and the children of different wives are distinguished by differences in the terms by which they address one another, own being distinguished from half-brothers. The practice occurs, or rather occurred, far less frequently in India, and is, of course, a widespread feature of Mohammedanism. It is frequent in Oceania, where, again, it is confined to the more important members of the community. In some parts of Melanesia it is the privilege of the old, while in Eddystone Island the practice is confined to chiefs, and to those who have taken ten heads in warfare.

Polyandry is far less frequent than polygyny, and, at the present time, flourishes most in certain parts of India. Two forms have been distinguished, that in which the several husbands of one woman are brothers, and that in which they are not related to one another. Since the first form occurs in Tibet, it was called Tibetan polyandry by McLennan, who was the first writer to utilize the custom in anthropological theory; but it is now more usual, and more satisfactory, to call it fraternal polyandry, or, if you object to the combination of words with these different derivations, adelphic polyandry. The second form was called by McLennan Nair polyandry, since the best known example occurred among the Nayars of Malabar, but it is more convenient to speak of it as non-fraternal polyandry. As a matter of fact, the Nayar form was of a rather complex kind, and it is doubtful whether it should be regarded as polyandry.[1]

The Nayar practice was to a large extent the result of a custom of the Nambutiri Brahmins of the country, who only allow the eldest son of each family to marry, the other sons consorting with Nayar women ; but as the children of these unions are Nayars, and stand in no definite social relations to their Nambutiri fathers, it is a question whether the practice should be regarded as marriage, at any rate if we regard marriage as, in its essence, an institution by means of which children are assigned the place which they are to occupy in the social community into which they are born.

The fraternal form occurs in Tibet, and, in a very pure form, among the Todas of the Nilgiri Hills in India, and occasionally elsewhere in India, especially in connexion with hypergamy, and I shall return to the practice in connexion with that mode of regulating marriage.

In other parts of the world polyandry has been recorded among a Bantu people, the purely pastoral Bahima,[2] and in Polynesia it occurs in the Marquesas Islands.[3] In ancient times it was described by Strabo and Cæsar as having been the custom of the Arabs and Britons. It is also said to have been practised by the Guanches of the Canary Islands, but in such cases it is difficult to be sure that the state recorded is genuine polyandry, and not some form of sexual communism.

The next form of marriage to be considered, the so-called group marriage, is one which presents great difficulties. In certain cases, as among the Todas of the Nilgiri Hills, polyandry has come to be combined with polygyny, probably as the result of an increase in the number of women, due to giving up the practice of female infanticide, which is usually combined with polyandry. If this were the only form of union in which

---

[1] Westermarck, *History of Human Marriage*, chap. xxix.
[2] id. iii, 191. J. Roscoe, *The Banyankole*, 1923, p. 123.
[3] Tautain, *L'Anthropologie*, vi, 644, 646, 648.

several husbands were united with several wives, the matter would be simple, and nothing more need be said about it. If we are to use the term " group-marriage ", with the meaning here attached to the term " group ", it ought to denote a form of marriage in which every male, or, at least, every male member of a generation of one group, is the husband of every female, or, at least, every woman of the corresponding generation of another group ; in which, further, the children are regarded as the children of the group, and not of any individual parent ; but we have no conclusive evidence that such a form of marriage exists, or has ever existed.

There are many aspects of marriage which I have not time to consider here, and must refer you either to Westermarck's *History of Human Marriage* or to my article in Hastings' *Encyclopædia*. I shall only refer briefly to two topics, infant marriage and marriage by capture. Infant marriage is best known as a practice of orthodox Hinduism ; but it also occurs in Melanesia and other parts of the world. In this form of marriage men, even old men, are betrothed or married to girls when these are infants, or even before they are born. The practice is often associated with a shortage of women, such as is produced by polygyny or female infanticide.

In Melanesia it is almost certainly due to the special form of polygamy, in which all the young women of the community are monopolized by the old men; while among the Todas it seems definitely to be connected with female infanticide. It is probably a widespread feature of human migrations that the migrating band has relatively few women, and if the migrants wish only to marry women of their own number, this would act as another source of the shortage of women and as a consequent motive for infant marriage. It is not improbable that this was the original motive for the infant marriage of the Hindus.

MODES OF CONTRACTING MARRIAGE

Marriage is contracted in various ways. The most frequent practice is one in which property of some kind is given as in return for husband or wife. In the latter case this property is usually called the bride-price ; in the former the bridegroom-price or dower.

It is important to note that when it is the custom to marry a relative, as in the cross-cousin marriage, no property passes, except in those cases in which the orthodox marriage does not take place, but some other woman is married. Another mode of arrangement is marriage by exchange, the most usual form being that in which brother and sister marry sister and brother. This practice may co-exist with marriage by purchase, and there is reason to believe that, in some cases, it is only a means of avoiding the expense attendant on the marriage payments.

Another mode is marriage by service, of which the well-known Old Testament case of Jacob is a good example.

Among some peoples marriage by elopement is so habitual that it may be regarded as a social institution. In all cases it seems to be due to obstacles to marriage, such as those attendant on excessive bride-price, or the monopoly of women by the old men.

The last mode I shall mention is marriage by capture, of which I may say a little more, because it has played a large part, an unduly large part, in speculations concerning the history of human society, especially in the work of McLennan and Robertson Smith. These speculations concerning marriage by capture were connected with the mistake of McLennan, to which I have already referred in this chapter, that exogamy was the custom of marrying out of the tribe. The capture of women from other tribes undoubtedly exists, but there is no evidence that it has taken any prominent part either in determining forms of social organization or features of the ritual of marriage. It is from features of this ritual, such as mock fights, that most of the evidence for the supposed wide prevalence of marriage by capture has been derived, but most of these customs are capable of a different explanation, and in some cases this different explanation is conspicuous. Thus, the prominent part taken by the cross-cousin of the bride in such ritual conflicts in Southern India leaves little doubt that the explanation is to be found in the former existence of the cross-cousin marriage. I have already mentioned that when a person other than her cross-cousin marries a girl he often had to satisfy her cross-cousin by some kind of payment, and the mock conflict is almost certainly only another form of recognition of his rights. I have advanced a similar explanation for the ritual capture of Melanesia, where this form of marriage was followed in order to evade the exclusive monopoly of the old men.

CHAPTER IV

KINSHIP AND RELATIONSHIP SYSTEMS

KINSHIP AND RELATIONSHIP SYSTEMS

MENTION has been made of those forms of domestic grouping which play a part in determining the place in society taken by a child. In a society such as ours, the only group of the kind is the family. On the other hand, among peoples with moieties or clans, who constitute the great majority of those of cultures of the lower order, there is a complex blend of social relationships dependent, not only on the family itself, which, so far as is known, is omnipresent in human society, but also on the moiety or clan. In different communities the parts played by these two forms of social grouping differ, and it is of the utmost importance, in the study of social organization, to distinguish between the relationships arising out of membership of the family from those arising out of membership of the moiety or clan. Since they are almost universally confused together under the heading of " kin " and " kinship ", it is first necessary to determine how to deal with this difficulty.

It will be remembered that, in order to get rid of the difficulty raised by the change which has taken place in the meaning of the word " clan ", Andrew Lang and Sir James Frazer have proposed to call the social group concerned a " kin " instead of a " clan ", but both of these writers continued to use " kin " and " kinship " as terms for relatives and relationships dependent on the family. It might be remarked here that one of the great difficulties of sociology, as of psychology, is that most of its technical terms are in general use in the speech of everyday life. It is a useful principle that, when a term in such general use is employed as a technical term, it shall be given a meaning as near that of the general usage as possible. There can be no doubt that the generally accepted meaning of the terms " kin " and " kinship " has reference to relationships dependent on the family, and, obeying the principle laid down, they will be used for relations of this kind.

It remains to find other terms for relations dependent on common membership of the moiety, clan, or sib. Many years ago I proposed that the word " sib ", which has now been adopted by Lowie as a term for the clan itself, should be used as a term corresponding to kin, but applying to clan relations in place of relations through the family. According to this usage members of a clan would be sib to one another, just as members of a family or kindred are said to be kin to one another, and the word " kinship " would have " sibship " as its equivalent when the clan or sib was in question (see p. 21).

With this distinction clear let us now consider more fully what we mean by kin and kinship. The first point to consider is whether these terms can be defined by means of blood-relationship or consanguinity. Among ourselves this usage would work perfectly well until we came to the practice of adoption, when it would break down; so, adoption being far more prevalent in many societies than among ourselves, this mode of defining kinship must be put on one side. In parts of Melanesia, for instance, the family to which a child belongs is not determined by the physiological act of birth, but depends on the performance of some social act ; in one island the man who pays the midwife becomes the father of the child and his wife becomes the mother ; in another the father is the man who plants a leaf of the cycas-tree before the door of the house. These are only dramatic examples of a widespread practice whereby fatherhood and motherhood depend, not on pro-creation and parturition, but on social convention, and it is evident that blood-relationship is quite inadequate as a means of defining kinship.

A second mode of defining kinship is by genealogical relation-ship other than by marriage. Every people of whom we have any exact knowledge, who have not destroyed their memories by learning to read and write, preserve their pedigrees, often in great completeness and extent. In general the relationships preserved in these pedigrees are those which actually determine the social relations of the different members of the community, and regulate their mutual duties and privileges towards one another, whether these functions have been determined by consanguinity or by some social procedure.[1]

A third mode of definition which has been suggested is by means of terms of relationship, but since these are determined by genealogical relationship and membership of the group, this is quite unsuitable.

A fourth method, formerly advocated by Dr. Malinowski, is by social function. Persons are regarded as kin to one another if their duties and privileges in relation to one another are those otherwise determined by consanguinity.

Of these four means by which kinship has been defined, I have not the slightest hesitation in choosing the second, that is, genealogical relationship, as at once the most exact and the most convenient. I define *kinship*, therefore, as relationship which is determined, and can be described, by means of genealogies.

According to this definition, kinship differs from relationship or sibship set up by membership of the moiety or clan, it being both wider and narrower in its scope, according to the point of view. The kin of a man are all his known relatives, both on the father's and the mother's side, who would belong to two different moieties or clans. In this way the kinship relationship is wider than the relationship set up by common membership of the moiety or clan which is unilateral. On the other hand, members of the moiety or clan with whom he could not trace relationship would not be kin in the sense in which the term is used in this book ; they would be sib, not kin.

Since every example of moiety or clan-organization

---

[1] Some instances of these functions will be discussed in this chapter (see p. 63 et seq.).

with which we are acquainted is combined with a family organization, many members of the clan would be kin as well as sib ; persons of other clans would be kin and not sib, and members of his clan with whom he could trace no genealogical relationship would be sib and not kin.

One advantage of defining kinship genealogically is that it excludes metaphorical relationship such as that which is concerned when we call a priest "father", any old woman "mother", or a fellow-clubman "brother", a usage which is very widespread throughout the world. Moreover, it only includes artificial relationship, such as blood-brotherhood, when this is so generally recognized as to become part of the social system, and rank with other modes of determining relationship as a means of regulating social duties and privileges.

To pass now to one of the most difficult topics with which we shall have to deal in this book, the terminology of relationship. In most writings on this subject, which follow the American ethnologist, Lewis Morgan, two chief modes of denoting relatives are distinguished, the so-called descriptive system and the so-called classificatory system. I shall distinguish a third, but will begin by considering the two varieties usually recognized.

I will begin with our own system, with which I can deal very briefly. In this system, which is of the same kind as all the other systems of Europe, with the doubtful exception of the Basque, we have terms, such as father, mother, brother and sister, used with great definiteness for the members of the family. The terms for relatives by marriage are not so definite, for the term brother-in-law may denote either the wife's brother or the sister's husband. All other relationships are grouped together under the three headings of uncle, aunt and cousin, which are used for relatives of the most diverse kind ; while cousin is used with a degree of looseness that would lead a Melanesian or an Australian to regard us as a hopelessly inexact and unscientific people. Following Morgan, this mode of nomenclature is known as descriptive. It is true that, except in the case of the family, our nomenclature is so loose that, if we wish to be exact, we have to use descriptive expressions such as mother's brother's son, father's sister's daughter, and so on, but one may have to do this with any system of nomenclature. Moreover, the terms uncle, aunt and cousin are just as classificatory as any terms of the so-called classificatory system, only with the difference that our classification is loose and inexact, in place of the strictly logical and exact nomenclature of the Australian or Melanesian savage.

The really characteristic feature of the European system is that the terms referring to the family are used exactly and with definite meanings, while all others are loose and inexact, and this is definitely connected with the preponderant importance of this family in our society. Our system is clearly dependent on the family (in the strict sense). I have proposed that it shall be called the *Family System*, and I shall adopt that term in this book.

THE CLASSIFICATORY SYSTEM

Just as the family has left its mark on the kinship systems of peoples among whom it is the predominant domestic group, so it is found that the moiety and clan have played their parts in determining relationship. A child born into a community with moieties or clans becomes a member of a domestic group other than the family in the strict sense ; and this is reflected in the terms of kinship that he addresses to those around him. The system of relationship found in these circumstances is called classificatory because whole groups of relatives are classed with the father, mother, brother, sister, and so forth, and receive the same terms of address. That is to say, relatives are grouped in classes. Thus, a person will give to a large number of men the term which he applies to his own father ; to a large class of women he gives the same name as that he uses for his mother ; and this applies even to the relationship of husband and wife. Thus, the distinctions of uncle, aunt, and cousin that play so fundamental a part in our system of relationship are largely obliterated in communities with moieties and clans.

I have carefully refrained from saying that a person has many fathers, mothers, wives, or husbands, and this avoidance should be observed unless a qualification is added indicat ng whether words are being used in the classificatory or the customary English sense. It must be recognized that in the classificatory system of relationship we are dealing, in the first place, with nomenclature; and in the second place I am obliged to say that a man gives to many persons the term he uses for his father, rather than that he has many fathers, because in a system of this kind there is no exact equivalent for any of our terms of relationship, and we have no equivalents for the terms of the classificatory system. In order to avoid such roundabout modes of expression I shall have to use our English terms in describing the system, but the context will, I think, make clear in every case whether I am using a word in our own or in the classificatory sense.

Before proceeding to consider the significance of the classificatory system, it will be well to glance at some of its general features.

A general characteristic of classificatory systems is that a man will call his father's brothers by the same term which he applies to his own father; also all his father's father's sons, i.e. his father's first cousins, in the male line, and his father's father's father's son's sons, i.e. his father's second cousins in the male line. Using our terms of relationship, he will denote as father a group consisting of the first, second (and third) cousins of his father in the male line. It is also an almost universal feature of the system that he will class with his father the husbands of his mother's sisters, and of all those whom the mother would call sister. But, in spite of this common nomenclature for so large a group of relatives, it must be realized that, so far as we know, every people who use the classificatory system of relationship distinguish the actual father, i.e. the social father, not necessarily the physiological father, from the other persons with whom he is classed ; but the persons grouped together as father may, on the other hand, be just as important as the real father in so far as social duties and privileges are concerned.

Just as numerous relatives are classed with the father, so all the mother's sisters are classed with the mother, and also her cousins according to the same rules as apply to the relationship of father, and the wives of all those who are called father are also classed with the mother. Every son of one called father or mother will be classed with the brothers, and every daughter of these persons with the sisters.

In the terminology of persons two generations removed there is more variety. In the simplest kind of system the father's father is classed with the mother's father, as among ourselves ; but in other cases the two are definitely distinguished from one another. Otherwise the classificatory rule holds good ; every man whom the father calls father will be classed with the actual father's father, and everyone whom the mother calls father will be classed with the actual mother's father.

What has just been said about the classificatory system refers to those with whom genealogical kinship can be traced. But the classificatory system belongs to peoples with moieties and clans, and, as is known, there are often many members of a clan with whom relationship cannot be traced. How do they come into the scheme of relationship ?   It is found that, wherever the classificatory system exists in association with a system of exogamous groups, the terms of relationship apply, not merely to relatives with whom it is possible to trace genealogical relationship, but also to all the members of a clan of a given generation, even if no such relationship with them can be traced. Thus, a man will not only apply the term " father " to all the brothers of his father, to all the son's sons of his father's father, to all the husbands of his mother's sisters and of his mother's mother's granddaughters, etc., but he will also apply the term to all the men of his father's clan of the same generation as his father, and to all the husbands of the women of the mother's clan of the same generation as the mother, even when it is quite impossible to show any genealogical relationship with them.[1]

The grouping together of relatives and members of clans and moieties is one of the chief characteristics of the classificatory system. In our own system it is true that relatives such as uncles, aunts, and cousins, are grouped together more or less indiscriminately, but we do at least distinguish members of our own family from other relatives. This is not the case with the classificatory system, which, as has just been shown, group many relatives with the actual parents, brothers, and sisters.

While the classificatory system of relationship may be defined as the system which groups together many relatives, and also members of the same moiety or clan, with actual members of the family, it is found that there are many varieties of terminology in respect of certain relatives. All through the classificatory system the groupings just described hold good, but this is not the case with certain other relatives, for instance, the mother's brother and the father's sister, and their children. On the contrary, more than one variation in the manner of their nomenclature may be mentioned. Some of these variations may be described, and then it will be possible to decide which are the most characteristic forms of the classificatory system.

In many classificatory systems relatives whom we group together are distinguished the one from the other. For instance, we group together father's and mother's brothers, and call them uncles. In many classificatory systems, on the other hand, the mother's brother is sharply distinguished from the father's brother. This applies, of course, not only to the actual mother's brother, but also to a large class of relatives of the mother's brother, his first, second, and third cousins, for instance.

[1] *Kinship and Social Organization*, pp. 70-1.

Supposing, for example, that the actual brothers of the actual mother are called *wadwam*, as in the island of Mabuiag in Torres Straits. Every man whom the mother calls brother will also be called *wadwam* by her son, and similarly every woman whom the father calls sister will be classed, as *ngaibat*, with the actual sisters of the actual father. Moreover, in the most characteristic form of the classificatory system, the children of those classed with the mother's brother and the father's sister are distinguished in nomenclature from the children of those whom the father calls brother and the mother calls sister. Thus these relatives fall into two groups. On the one side are the father's brothers and mother's sisters, who are classed with the father and mother, while their children are classed with the actual brothers and sisters. In the other group are the mother's brothers and the father's sisters, whose children are classed together, but are clearly separated in nomenclature from the brothers and sisters. Relatives whom we group together as uncles, aunts, and cousins, for instance, fall into two sharply defined groups.

A variation from this system which I will mention is one which is of not infrequent occurrence, in which, although the mother's brother and the father's sister are distinguished from the father's brother and the mother's sister, their children are all classed together. In this form of the system those we call uncles and aunts fall into two groups, but there is agreement with our own procedure in classing all first cousins together. Morgan believed that these differences served to distinguish the classificatory systems of North America from those of Asia, and named them accordingly ; but later work has shown that this is not so.

Another variety is more important. The variation in which the children of the father's brother, father's sister, mother's brother and mother's sister are all classed together seems to be only an intermediate step towards a form of the classificatory system in which the father's brother is classed with the mother's brother and the father's sister with the mother's sister. The result is to produce a system of great simplicity, in which all persons of the generation of the speaker with whom any genealogical relationship, other than by marriage, can be traced, are classed with the brothers and sisters. All persons of the preceding generation are classed with the father or mother ; all of the succeeding generation with sons or daughters ; and all related persons of the generations once removed are classed with the grandparent or grandchild. This system was by Morgan called the Malayan system ; but, as later knowledge has made it very doubtful whether it is used by the Malays, the term is not happy. This kind of system is characteristic of the Polynesians, and, as it was first described in the Hawaiian Islands, it is now usually known as the Hawaiian system.

It would be possible, by comparing various classificatory systems of relationship, to range them in an order of complexity. Some of these. systems, as has been seen, are richer in their terminology than others, and make finer distinctions between relatives. The poorest of all systems is the Hawaiian, which has just been mentioned. Morgan supposed it to be the starting-point of the system.

This view may be criticized from three points of view. In the first place the Polynesian system of denoting relationship does not apply to the society as a whole. The Hawaiian does not regard every other Hawaiian of his generation as a brother or sister, but only applies these terms to those with whom he can trace genealogical relationship. That is, the use of the term implies the existence of genealogies based on individual marriage.

In the second place, the Hawaiian usage does not imply absence of knowledge of parenthood, but is simply the result of the existence of the bilateral mode of grouping, which I have called a kindred.

Thirdly, Morgan supposed that the Polynesians were an example of a primitive people, basing this view on the simplicity of their material arts, especially as shown by the absence of pottery. Morgan's opinion was perhaps excusable in the state of knowledge of Polynesian society of his day, but we now know that the Polynesians are a highly developed people intellectually, and have social institutions, and especially political institutions, of an advanced kind. The rudeness of their material culture is a result of their simple environment in Oceanic islands. There is little doubt that their ancestors made pottery, and that this art disappeared, perhaps, as the result of the paucity of suitable material ; and many of us are coming to believe that these ancestors were also acquainted with metal-working.[1] The Polynesians are a people among whom we should expect to find late, rather than early, patterns of social institution. Morgan's view is thus based on a complete misunderstanding of both Polynesian relationship and of Polynesian culture in general, and can be put aside as having no foundation. Since the least complicated system of Oceania belongs to a highly developed people such as the Hawaiians, it is probable that the most complicated systems, such as those of the Dieri of Australia and of Pentecost Island, represent the starting-point of the system, and that, by a process of gradual simplification, the Hawaiian system has been reached, in which the relationship system is apparently based on the kindred form of grouping.

I have said earlier that a third variety of system of relationship can be distinguished. It occurs in the most characteristic form among Semitic and Nilotic peoples, and is much more truly descriptive than either of the other systems we have considered. Thus, in the Arabic system of Egypt the father's brother being *amn*, the son of the father's brother is *ibn amn*, and his daughter *bint amn*. Again, the mother's brother being *khal*, the mother's brother's son is *ibn khal*, and his daughter *bint khal*, and so on. I do not propose to say more about this system here, and will only point out that it is associated with the special form of social grouping I have

---

[1] See Perry, *The Children of the Sun*, s.v. Hawaii, for further information on this topic.

called the kindred, and I have suggested that it may be called the *kindred system*.[1]

It is now time to turn to other features of systems of relationship, and particularly of the classificatory system.   In this the use of terms often varies with the sex of the speaker. Men and women use different terms when addressing a person with whom, from our point of view, they stand in the same relation. The most striking instance of this occurs in the nomenclature for brother and sister.   In many forms of the classificatory system two brothers use a term for one another which is also used between two sisters, but brother and sister employ a wholly different term, which is used reciprocally.   I will give an instance from Torres Straits.   In the island of Mabuiag a man calls his brother *tukoiab*, and this word is also used by a woman when addressing her sister.   When a man is addressing his sister, on the other hand, he calls her *babat*, and this term is used reciprocally when the sister addresses her brother. One way of putting this difference is that the system denotes relationship as well as the relatives ; there is a word for the relationship between brothers, a word for the relationship between sisters, and another word for the relationship between brother and sister.   This principle of nomenclature, which is different from our own, runs through the whole system.   The result is that our terms brother and sister are quite untranslatable ; as we have no exact equivalent for the Mabuiag terms we can only adopt the circumlocution " brother, man speaking " and " brother, woman speaking ", " sister, man speaking ", and " sister, woman speaking ".   One result of this is that if you are discussing relationships with a native in English and he uses the word brother or sister, you have to ask him whether he is referring to a man or a woman, and the only satisfactory plan is to use the native terms.

A feature of the classificatory system, closely related to the usage just considered, is that its terms are often used

---

[1] Cf. (Mrs.) B. Z. Seligman, " Studies in Semitic Kinship " : *Bull. Sch. of Oriental Studies*, iii, London, 1923.

reciprocally. Thus, the relationship of uncle and nephew, to use our own words, may have only one term connected with it, instead of the two of our own language and of many classificatory systems. To take an example I have already mentioned, the word *wadwam* is not only applied in the island of Mabuiag to the mother's brother, but is also used by the senior member of the relationship when addressing his nephew. We might say that *wadwam* is an inclusive term for the relationship of uncle and nephew, just as in the same island *babat* is an inclusive term for the relationship of brother and sister. More rarely a similar character applies to the nomenclature for grandparent and grandchild. A child applies to his grandfather precisely the same term which the grandfather gives to him, and a similar feature is even more frequent in the nomenclature for relatives by marriage.

The classificatory system has a feature in that brothers and sisters, own and classificatory, are often distinguished from one another according to age. A man will apply one term to brothers older than himself and a different term to his younger brothers, the same rule holding good of the terms used between sisters, own and classificatory. The distinction may also be made in the terms used between brother and sister, except in the case of the reciprocal usage, when this distinction of nomenclature according to age does not apply to the mutual relationship of brother and sister.

A similar distinction according to age is also frequently made between the elder and younger brothers, own and classificatory, of the father, and more rarely between the elder and younger sisters of the mother, this usage occurring especially among matrilineal peoples.

I have so far considered the classificatory system as a system of nomenclature. It was once supposed, especially by those who had no first-hand acquaintance with the subject, that it was a mere collection of terms of address. It is now thoroughly established, however, that these terms connote definite social functions, specific duties, privileges, and restrictions on conduct,

and that these social functions apply to relatives in the classificatory sense, as well as to relatives in the much narrower sense
which the terms would bear among ourselves. Thus, there are
many peoples among whom there is a special relation between
a man and his mother's brother. The nephew has certain
definite duties in relation to his uncle, and has certain privileges,
including the use of his property, amounting in some cases to
a state of affairs in which all property is common to the two.
These social relations do not apply merely to the actual brother
of the own mother, but to all those whom the mother calls
brother, though in most cases the nearer relationship of the
actual mother's brother is recognized, and the various social
functions more strictly observed. To take one example, among
those peoples where a man has the right to marry the widow
of the mother's brother, or even to take her as a wife while his
uncle is alive, the right applies to the wives of all those whom
his mother would call brother, though the right is more likely
to be satisfied the nearer the actual genealogical relationship
of the two.

Moreover, the more thoroughly we investigate the nomenclature of the classificatory system, the more universal do we
find the rule that its terms have a meaning and carry with
them distinctions of social function. Thus, the distinction
between father's brother and mother's brother is not merely
correlated with the fact that in the clan organization the two
persons distinguished in nomenclature must necessarily belong
to different moieties or clans, but they have social functions
wholly different from one another ; while in those systems,
such as that of the Hawaiians, where relatives are not so
distinguished in nomenclature, we find also an absence of
distinctions of social function.

We are still, however, in much uncertainty concerning the
exact significance of some of the distinctions I have described,
such as the feature of reciprocity and the distinction according
to age. It is noteworthy that, in some of the cases where there
is reciprocity of nomenclature, there is also reciprocity of social

function. Thus, in Mabuiag the reciprocal relationship of *wadwam* carries with it reciprocity in the ownership of property. The two relatives theoretically, if not actually, have their property in common.

Again, in some parts of the world a definite distinction is made between elder and younger brothers in connexion with the levirate, the practice according to which a widow is taken by her husband's brother. In India and elsewhere the widow may only be taken by her late husband's younger brother, and, as Mr. Chatterji has shown in a paper not yet published, this distinction of social function in India is definitely correlated with a corresponding distinction in nomenclature.

The social duties, privileges, and restrictions which are imposed upon classificatory relatives by traditional custom are of the most varied kinds. They include the duty of mutual helpfulness, either in general, or on special occasions such as funeral and other rites ; privileges, especially in connexion with property ; and restrictions of many kinds. A most important group of the last kind may be classed together as customs of avoidance. Social regulations are frequent, according to which the names of certain relatives may not be mentioned, or the relatives themselves may not be spoken to, at any rate, familiarly. In other cases these relatives may not see or be in the presence of one another, and, in one case I have recorded, this avoidance was so strict that it continued after death, a person who had avoided a relative throughout life was not permitted to enter the house in which she lay dead.

The relative to whom these customs of avoidance apply most frequently is the mother-in-law, or, more strictly, the wife's mother, for the avoidance of her parents-in-law by a woman is less frequent and usually less strict. Avoidance between brothers- and sisters-in-law is less frequent. An interesting case is avoidance between brother and sister, which may be very strict, the extreme case of avoidance after death which I have quoted having applied to these relatives.

There is little doubt that these customs of avoidance are

F

connected in many cases with the potentiality of sexual relations ; two relatives to whom sexual relations are forbidden have to avoid one another altogether. Moreover, there is little doubt that, where relatives now avoid one another, sexual relations were formerly allowed, if they were not habitual, and the theoretical interest of these customs arises out of this possibility. Much of the evidence for the former prevalence of group-marriage or organized sexual communism is derived from customs of this kind.

It is clear, however, that sexual relations do not furnish a complete explanation of these customs, for they frequently occur between members of the same sex. It is possible that in these cases customs of avoidance are associated with the dual organization, the avoidance between men being due to the fact that they belong to hostile moieties.[1]

In two parts of the world, Melanesia and North America, customs of the opposite kind have been recorded, in which familiarity between certain relatives is obligatory. Such relatives should not meet without joking or without making opprobrious or obscene remarks at the expense of the other. In the Banks Islands, the relative towards whom this obligation is most pronounced is the husband of the father's sister ; but where the custom is expressed between persons of different sex there is reason to believe that it is associated with ideas in reference to group marriage or sexual communism. In North America brothers- and sisters-in-law are prominent among the relatives with whom it is obligatory to joke.

THE CLASSIFICATORY SYSTEM AND THE DUAL ORGANIZATION

(i) *Near kin*

When considering the main features of the classificatory system of relationship, the system which accompanies moieties and clans, it was found that certain relatives whom we distinguish the one from the other were grouped together, while

---

[1] *History of Melanesian Society*, ii, 135.

others whom we grouped together were differentiated. The grouping with parents, for instance, of relatives whom we distinguish from parents is to be explained by the fact that the people using such terms of relationship are the members of a moiety or clan, and tend to group all members of the same generation together, whether genealogical relationship between them can be established or not. But the feature of the classificatory system whereby relatives whom we group together are distinguished has yet to be explained in detail.

The matter is not so simple as might at first sight appear. It is evident that the distinction between the mother's brother and the father's brother, between the mother's sister and the father's sister is to be explained by the exogamy of either the clan or the moiety, for this would cause the parents to belong to different clans, or moieties, as well as their brothers and sisters. As the result of a marriage between members of two different clans, there would ensue the grouping of mother's and father's relatives in two distinct bodies ; the mother's brother will belong to one group, and the father's brother will belong to another distinct group. They are distinguished from one another in this way, and according as descent is matrilineal or patrilineal the one or the other will be nearer in relationship to their nephew. If descent be matrilineal, then the mother's brother will belong to the same group as his nephew, while the father will belong to another group. Thus the distinction between near kin can be explained on the basis of the moiety or clan system that always accompanies them.

If it were only a question of the distinction between those relatives just mentioned, the origin of the classificatory system might be sought in either the dual organization or in the clan system.[1] But certain distinctions between relatives suggest strongly that the dual organization was the sole source of this system of relationship, and that, consequently, the clan grouping only enters incidentally into the matter. It is an

[1] See Ghuyre, " Dual Organization in India " : *Journ. Roy. Anthr. Inst.*, liii, 1923.

almost universal feature of the classificatory system that the children of brothers are classed with the children of sisters. A man applies the same terms to his mother's sister's children which he uses for his father's brother's children, and the use of this term, being the same as that used for a brother or sister, carries with it the most rigorous prohibition of marriage. Such a condition would not follow necessarily from a social state in which there were more than two social groups. If the society were patrilineal, the children of two brothers would necessarily belong to the same social group, so that the principle of exogamy would prevent marriage between them, but if the women of the group had married into different clans, there is no reason arising out of the principle of exogamy which should prevent marriage between their children, or lead to the use of a term common to them and the children of brothers. Similarly, if the society were matrilineal, the children of two sisters would necessarily belong to the same social group, but this would not be the case with the children of brothers, who might marry into different social groups.

If, however, there be only two social groups, the case is very different. It would make no difference whether descent were patrilineal or matrilineal. In each case the children of two brothers or of two sisters must belong to the same moiety, while the children of brother and sister must belong to different moieties. The children of two brothers would be just as ineligible as consorts as the children of two sisters. Similarly, it would be a natural consequence of the dual organization that the mother's brother's children should be classed with the father's sister's children, but this would not be necessary if there were more than two social groups.[1]

(ii) Relatives by Marriage

The conclusion that the classificatory system of relationship is dependent on the dual organization by no means explains all its features. There are yet other mechanisms at work. As

[1] *History of Melanesian Society*, ii, p. 16.

has been found before, the kinship group plays its part in all regulations of marriage, and it is found that kinship is important in the classificatory system. For another feature of the classificatory system has yet to be explained, namely, the identity that is found in many systems between the terms of address applied to near kin and relatives by marriage. Suppose it to happen that, in a given community, the same term is applied to a man's mother's brother, the husband of his father's sister, and his father-in-law ; while his father's sister, his mother's brother's wife, and his mother-in-law are grouped together. Again, suppose that, in the same system, an identical term is applied, not only to the child of the mother's brother or the father's sister who differs in sex from the speaker, but also to the wife's sister and the brother's wife, in the case of a man, and to the husband's brother and sister's husband in the case of a woman.

The fact that relatives by marriage are classed with near kin at once suggests marriage of a certain kind, which transforms the mother's brother into the father-in-law, and so on. Obviously to transform the mother's brother into a father-in-law it is necessary to marry his daughter, your cousin, cross-cousin as it is termed. By this form of marriage you will have effected all the other correspondences that have been mentioned, as is evident from the diagram. Consulting this diagram, suppose that C marries d.[1]

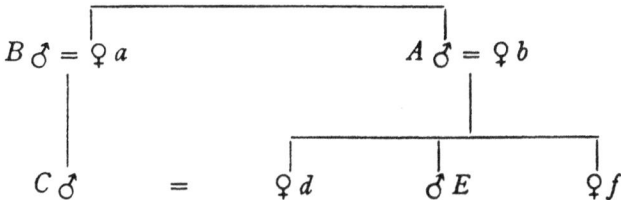

$$B \, \male = \female \, a \qquad\qquad A \, \male = \female \, b$$

$$C \, \male \qquad = \qquad \female \, d \qquad \male \, E \qquad \female \, f$$

In this case it is evident that the mother's brother, A, becomes C's father-in-law, while b, the wife of the mother's brother, becomes his mother-in-law. Reciprocally, C, who

---

[1] Capitals stand for men, small letters for women.

before his marriage had been the sister's son of *A* and the husband's sister's son of *b*, now becomes their son-in-law. Further, *E* and *f*, the other children of *A* and *b*, who before the marriage had been only the cousins of *C*, now become his wife's brother and sister. Similarly, *a*, who before the marriage of *d* was her father's sister, now becomes also her husband's mother, and *B*, her father's sister's husband, comes to stand in the relationship of husband's father ; if *C* should have any brothers and sisters, these cousins would now become brothers- and sisters-in-law. Other combinations of relationship that exist in classificatory systems can be shown to result from the cross-cousin marriage. If this marriage be an established institution, the relationships of mother's brother and father's sister's husband will come to be combined in one and the same person, and there will be a similar combination of the relationships of father's sister and mother's brother's wife.

If it can be shown that the cross-cousin marriage is, or has been, practised in communities that possess such characteristics in their classificatory system of relationship, then it will follow that these relationship equations are presumably the outcome of this form of marriage. This has been shown to be the case in *The History of Melanesian Society*.

" In many places where we know the cross-cousin marriage to be an established institution, we find just those common designations which I have just described. Thus, in the Mbau dialect of Fiji the word *vungo* is applied to the mother's brother, the husband of the father's sister and the father-in-law. The word *nganei* is used for the father's sister, the mother's brother's wife and the mother-in-law. *Ndavola* is used not only for the child of the mother's brother or father's sister when differing in sex from the speaker, but this word is also used by a man for his wife's sister and his brother's wife, and by a woman for her husband's brother and her sister's husband. Every one of these details of the Mbau system is the direct and inevitable consequence of the cross-cousin marriage, if it become an established and habitual practice.

" The Fijian system does not stand alone in Melanesia. In the southern islands of the New Hebrides, in Tanna, Eromanga, Anaiteum, and Aniwa, the cross-cousin marriage is practised and their systems of relationship have features similar to those of Fiji. Thus, in Anaiteum the word *matak* applies to the mother's brother, the father's sister's husband and the father-in-law, while the word *engak* used for the cross-cousin is not only used for the wife's sister and the brother's wife, but also for the wife herself.

" Again, in the island of Guadalcanar in the Solomons the system of relationship is just such as would result from the cross-cousin marriage. One term, *nia*, is used for the mother's brother and the wife's father, and probably also for the father's sister's husband and the husband's father . . . Similarly, *tarunga* includes in its connotation the father's sister, the mother's brother's wife, and the wife's mother, while the word *iva* is used for both cross-cousins and brothers- and sisters-in-law. Corresponding to this terminology there seemed to be no doubt that it was the custom for a man to marry the daughter of his mother's brother or his father's sister . . ."

" These three regions, Fiji, the southern New Hebrides, and Guadalcanar, are the only parts of Melanesia included in my survey where I found the practice of the cross-cousin marriage, and in all three regions the systems of relationship are just such as would follow from this form of marriage." [1]

This establishes, for Melanesia at least, a correspondence between certain features of the classificatory system and the cross-cousin marriage. In like manner, as may be seen by a reference to *The History of Melanesian Society* or *Kinship or Social Organization*, other marriages between relatives have had their effect on the nomenclature of relationship systems of peoples with the dual or clan organization. One more instance of this kind may perhaps be of interest.

It may sound absurd to think that a man could marry his

---

[1] *Kinship and Social Organization*, pp. 22 sqq.

granddaughter, yet there is no doubt that this is, or was, the practice in more than one part of the world. The people of Pentecost in the New Hebrides possess a bizarre and complex system of relationship that seems to have no sense in it at all. They actually group together in one category certain relatives two generations apart. For instance, the mother's mother has the same designation as the elder sister ; the wife's mother as the daughter ; the wife's brother as the daughter's son. It had been found that, in the New Hebrides, marriages took place between relatives one generation apart, so these facts suggested that, in Pentecost, grandparents married their grandchildren, that marriages took place between relatives two generations apart. The mystery was solved by John Pantatun, a native of Bank's Islands, who helped much in the collection of material for *The History of Melanesian Society*. He was fond of comparing his own island and the island of Pentecost. " One day he let fall the observation with just such a manner as that in which we so often accuse neighbouring nations of ridiculous or disgusting practices, ' O ! Raga ! That is the place where they marry their granddaughters.' " [1] This gave the clue, and it was found, on examination of the relationship system of Pentecost (Raga), that the features of the system could be explained on the basis of a marriage between a man and his brother's granddaughter.

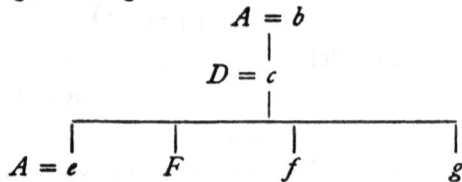

$$A = b$$
$$|$$
$$D = c$$
$$|$$

$$A = e \qquad F \qquad f \qquad g$$

The diagram shows some of the consequences of this form of marriage. If A marries e, c, who previous to the marriage had been only the daughter of A, now becomes also his wife's mother ; and D, who had previously been his daughter's husband, now becomes his wife's father. Similarly, F, who before the new marriage was the daughter's son of A, now

[1] *Kinship and Social Organization*, p. 34.

becomes the brother of his wife, while *f*, his daughter's daughter, becomes his wife's sister. Lastly, if we assume that it would be the elder daughter of the daughter who would be married by their grandfathers, *e*, who before the marriage had been the elder sister of *F* and *f*, now comes through her marriage to occupy the position of their mother's mother."

"When, after making these deductions, I examined my record of the Pentecost terms, I found that its terminology corresponded exactly with those which had been deduced. The wife's mother and the daughter were both called *nitu*. The daughter's husband and the wife's father were both called *bwaliga*. The daughter's children were called *mabi*, and this term was also used for the brother and sister of a wife. Lastly, the mother's mother was found to be classed with the elder sister, both being called *tuaga*." [1]

Other instances could be adduced to show how certain forms of marriage have evidently had their influence on relationship systems. For these the reader is referred to the works already mentioned. It is now necessary to inquire into the meaning of these marriages between relatives. The regular forms of marriage that characterize people with the classificatory system of relationship are with the daughter of the mother's brother or the father's sister, the cross-cousin marriage ; with the brother's daughter ; with the wife of the mother's brother ; with the daughter's daughter ; with the daughter of the sister's son, and so on.

It can be shown that most marriages between relatives are to be explained on the hypothesis that they originated in a society based on the dual organization with matrilineal descent, in which it was essential to marry somebody belonging to the opposite moiety. The moiety is a unilateral form of grouping, and descent is usually through the mother. So if we consider what would happen in a group of kindred in a dual society, we shall see who are possible mates, and who are forbidden.

[1] Op. cit., pp. 35-6.

```
 |‾‾‾‾‾‾|            |‾‾‾‾‾‾‾|              |‾‾‾‾‾‾‾‾‾|
A = b    B = a       A = b     B = a       B = a      A = b
 |        |          |‾‾‾‾‾|‾‾‾‾‾‾|          |          |
 b        a        B = a   B   A = b        a          b
                    |            |‾‾‾‾|
                  B = a          b    B = a
                    |                   |
                    a                   a
```

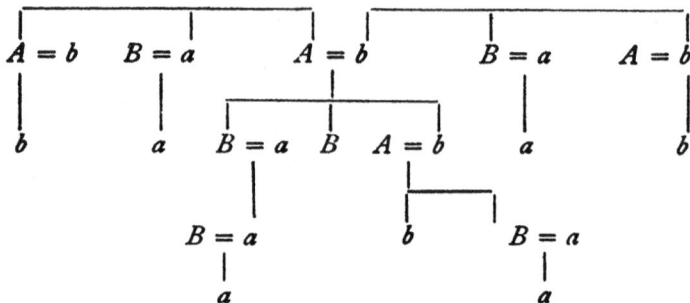

The diagram represents a man, B, together with certain of his relatives. They will all belong either to A or to B moiety, and the women who are a will be possible mates.

So B may marry his father's father's wife, his father's sister, his mother's brother's wife, his mother's brother's daughter, his brother's daughter, and his brother's daughter's daughter. Thus he may marry, on the basis of the dual organization, exactly those relatives whom we find him marrying in the case of peoples with the classificatory system of relationship. [1] This explains how it is that near kin

[1] [The following quotations from Rivers's other works will make it quite clear that this was his interpretation of the facts. He says that " there are certain features of the classificatory system which suggest its origin in a special form of exogamous social grouping, viz., that usually known as the dual system in which there are two social groups or moieties " (*The History of Melanesian Society*, ii, 72 ; see also 82). Again, " with one exception, I have been quite unable to conceive any mechanism whereby the marriages in question could have arisen out of a system in which there were more than two groups " (op. cit., p. 66). He also says " If my argument be accepted, it is clear that the dual organization with matrilineal descent was the essential element of the social structure at the earliest period to which the evidence leads us ".

" In all those places where the evidence for the existence of anomalous forms of marriage is definite, the dual organization with matrilineal descent must have been so vitally important that it is not easy to see how there can have been room for any other social mechanism. The whole scheme of development I have traced would only be possible if the dual organization forced men and women into these forms of marriage. Among the Dieri of Australia at the present time the dual organization and a totemic system exist side by side, and the possibility cannot be excluded that such a condition may also have been present at that stage of the history of Melanesian society to which the study of systems of relationship has led us. But it is clear that if such a totemic organization were combined with the dual organization, it played no essential part in the regulation of marriage " (*Mel. Soc.*, p. 83).

are identified in classificatory relationship systems with relatives by marriage. The system at work is one of marriage with near kin, which turns other relatives by birth into relatives by marriage. It must clearly be understood that, in order that the classificatory system could acquire these features, these forms of marriage must have been universal, not sporadic.

Corroborative evidence for this conclusion is provided by the work of A. R. Brown in Australia, who shows that throughout the greater part of the continent the systems of relationship are based on two chief forms of marriage, the cross-cousin marriage, and marriage between a man and the daughter's daughter of his mother's mother's brother, a kind of cross-cousin, these marriages usually being with near kin. Some Australian tribes only have two moieties, and these are connected with marriage ; in others these two marriage classes are split into two, giving four marriage classes; in others again they are split into eight. But, whether there be two, four, or eight classes regulating marriage, the two rules are equally effective.

There are other explanations of the origin of the cross-cousin marriage besides that which makes it the consequence of the dual organization, and the possibility of other modes of explanation must be kept in mind. For, although in Melanesia and Australia the two institutions exist side by side, in other parts of the world, Africa for instance, the cross-cousin marriage exists with no direct evidence in favour of the dual organization.[1] If the explanation be accepted, then it would follow that the dual organization must have had a wider distribution than it now has. In this connexion it must be

---

" In all those places, then, where we have evidence of the existence of marriage with the daughter's daughter and with the wives of the father's father and mother's brothers we may conclude that the dual organization with matrilineal descent was the older form of social organization and the other forms are later." (Ibid., pp. 83–4.)]

[1] [Except, of course, that the dual organization seems to have existed among the Gallas and Ovambo.]

remembered, however, that the Gallas had some sort of dual division with intermarriage. [Since the Bantu peoples came from the north-east, it is possible that they derived their cross-cousin marriage from some such source.]

A second explanation of the cross-cousin marriage is that it is a secondary consequence of the transition from mother-right to father-right. In mother-right a man's property goes to his sister's child, but when the change to father-right took place property would pass to his children, and it has been supposed that the conflict with vested interests was avoided by a marriage in which a man kept inheritance, to some extent at least, in the old channel, by marrying his sister's son, who was the former inheritor under mother-right, to his daughter.

In addition to certain difficulties, to the consideration of which I hope to return later, neither this kind of interpretation nor the derivation from the dual organization provide an explanation of the varieties of the cross-cousin marriage ; why in some places it should be the custom for a man to marry the daughter of his mother's brother, and in others the daughter of his father's sister.

These variations are accounted for by a mechanism which I have recorded from Melanesia. In several parts of this region it is orthodox for a man to marry the wife of his mother's brother. A man gives his wife, or one of his wives, to his sister's son. When in the Torres Islands I was told that sometimes a man would give his daughter in place of his wife, and the resulting marriage would, of course, be one in which the sister's son would be marrying his mother's brother's daughter. In other parts of Melanesia it is the practice to marry the father's sister, and, if the father's sister gave her daughter in place of herself, we should have that form of the cross-cousin marriage in which a man marries the daughter of his father's sister.

I have only advanced this mechanism to explain the cross-cousin marriages of Melanesia. Its adoption for other parts of the world involve a much more extensive distribution of the marriage with the mother's brother's wife and with the father's sister than we have any evidence to support at present. I mention this explanation partly to illustrate these peculiar forms of marriage, and their relation to one another, partly to give an idea of the possible importance of these forms of marriage in the reconstruction of the past history of social organization.[1]

The nature of the classificatory system has now been made fairly clear. It depends upon kinship and sibship, upon the membership of a family and of a moiety or clan. Again, certain of its features are only to be explained as the outcome of the dual organization of society in which it was obligatory for certain relatives to marry. It is quite certain that, in Australia for instance, certain marriages between relatives, principally the cross-cousin marriage, were the only forms of marriage that could be constructed, that, speaking generally, other forms of marriage simply did not exist. The final problem, therefore, is that of determining how it came about that, in the dual organization, certain marriages between near kin were made obligatory.[2]

History of Marriage

I am now in a position to consider the speculations concerning the history of marriage which are so prominent in sociological writings, and I will begin with those associated with the name of the American ethnologist, Lewis H. Morgan. According to this writer, marriage has evolved by a gradual process from a state of primitive promiscuity through an intermediate stage of group-marriage. It is not, I think, generally recognized that this hypothesis arose entirely out of the consideration of kinship, and especially out of the study of the various forms of the classificatory system of which Morgan was the discoverer. He started from the Hawaiian, or, as he called

---

[1] [It is obvious, of course, that the explanation of marriage between blood relatives must be one that will account for the general principle, and that it is dangerous to argue from one case alone.]

[2] See Appendix III for a further consideration of these matters.

it, the Malayan system, and supposed it to be the original and most primitive mode of denoting relationship. In this system, as may be seen from the table published by Morgan, all the members of the group of the same generation regard themselves as brothers and sisters, and Morgan supposed that this signified that the society out of which it arose was completely promiscuous, so that, in the absence of any form of marriage, children were regarded as the progeny of the society as a whole.

There is no reason to believe that Morgan's theory of an original promiscuity is correct. On the contrary, as has already been shown, his initial assumption that the Hawaiians represent a primitive stage of human society is entirely unfounded. For the group-marriage, or organized sexual communism, which Morgan supposed to be an intermediate phase between promiscuity and monogamy, there is more evidence.[1] Many features of the classificatory system of relationship, otherwise difficult to understand, become readily explicable if they grew out of a state of society in which a group of men had a group of wives in common. Thus, in many forms of the classificatory system, a man classes with his own wife in nomenclature all those women whom his wife would call " sister " in the classificatory sense, and in some cases there is definite evidence that this is not an empty system of terms of address, but implies relations with these women corresponding with those of the wife in the limited sense. Correspondingly, in the same systems, a woman classes with her husband all those men whom her husband calls brother ; and again there is evidence, in some cases, at least, that this nomenclature is more than a barren form. In Melanesia traces of sexual communism are especially strong in those parts which have the dual organization.

Moreover, in certain societies, there is no question as to the existence of organized sexual communism similar to that of group-marriage, though, in these cases, the group concerned is not the moiety or clan but a special kind of group called an

[1] See chaps. xxi and xxxii of *The History of Melanesian Society.*

age-class. Thus, in one part of New Guinea, all the men born within a given period of time form a group, the members of which have various social relationships, duties, privileges, etc., to one another, and among these relations is one that, though each individual member may have an individual wife, she is shared with all the other members of the age-grade. A similar custom exists in Africa among such peoples as the Masai, but in that continent it is usually men who have been circumcised together, rather than those born within a given period of time, who form the age-grade with its communistic practices. It must be remembered that these age-grades are specialized forms of grouping only known to exist in a few parts of the world, but they show that sexual group-relations form a potentiality of human nature which we have got to accept, however repugnant they may be to our sentiments and traditions. We need more evidence before we should make up our minds concerning the existence of group-marriage as a regular feature of the history of human society. Even if its existence in the case of the clan can be proved, or if it can be shown to be, or to have been, a widespread practice, it need not follow that it has been universal among mankind and has formed a constant feature of the evolution of human society. I may point out, however, that the classificatory system has a very extensive distribution. If many of its most characteristic features have arisen out of a system of group-marriage or organized sexual communism, this practice must also have been at one time or another widely prevalent among mankind.

Even if we accept the occurrence of group-relations as a feature of the history of marriage, it does not follow that it was the earliest phase in this history ; and, indeed, there is much reason to believe that it was not, but that it arose as part of a special development. We are still almost entirely in the stage of pure speculation concerning the earlier phases of the history of human society, and the sketch I am about to give must be regarded merely as a suggestion. There is much reason to believe that the earliest stage was one, which may be called the collecting stage, in which men lived together in small groups, possibly corresponding closely to the family, but of a loose, ill-defined kind which may be called a band. Such a society is still found among the Andamanese and other peoples.

When man has to live by collecting wild fruits and roots, grubs, and small game, he has to work over a large area to obtain sustenance, and the social group must necessarily be small in size with a relatively large area as its hunting ground. Large aggregations of human beings would not merely serve no social purpose, but would even be prejudicial to welfare. If, however, agriculture arises, or is introduced, among such a people, it will become possible for a large group to support itself on an area which formerly was only sufficient for one about the size of a family. Moreover, the need for the protection of their cultivated ground from the predations of animals or of other human groups would make the formation of large groups serviceable. It would provide a motive for much larger associations than were possible in the collecting stage. There is reason to believe that through some such process the clan organization grew out of the loosely organized band of the collecting stage.

If the evidence of the classificatory system is to be trusted, these larger aggregations came to practise sexual communism, which developed into an organized system. Just how this happened we have at present little means for telling, and until we are more certain concerning the former existence of a communistic stage it is perhaps hardly worth speculating concerning the mode of its appearance. I should only like to emphasize again the fact that we have clear evidence that existing varieties of mankind practise sexual communism, and man must therefore have tendencies in that direction.[1] If such tendencies were present during the collecting stage, but through the smallness and isolation of the social group

---

[1] [There is no inherent necessity in this point of view. It is possible, on the contrary, that sexual communism could have arisen as a reaction to some social institution.]

found no opportunity for expression, it is not unnatural that the growth of larger communities living peacefully together should have given such opportunity which, in many parts of the world, not necessarily everywhere, became the starting-point of a system of group-marriage.

Another frequent speculation concerning the history of human marriage assigns an important place to polyandry as a stage in its development. One of the chief pioneers in the study of the history of marriage was J. F. McLennan, and it is the importance which he attached to polyandry which has given this form of marriage a prominent place in discussions on marriage, a prominence emphasized by the studies of Robertson Smith on Semitic society.[1]

At the present time it is clear that polyandry is an exceptional practice (see p. 43). There are, as has been mentioned, ancient records of its existence among the peoples of the near East, and in the Canary Islands ; while it is probable that the record by Cæsar of this form of marriage among the Britons has taken a definite part in giving polyandry the prominence it has attained in our sociological speculations. It is not improbable that some of the ancient records rest on faulty observation of some kind of sexual communism, the sharing of a wife by several men having attracted more attention than other features of the communistic practices.

A more important cause of the prominence given to polyandry, which goes back to McLennan, is that the practice known as the levirate has been misunderstood. In this practice a widow is taken as wife by the deceased husband's brother, and this has been regarded by McLennan, Robertson Smith, and many others as a survival of polyandry. The practice has many varieties, the form with which we are especially familiar through its description in the Old Testament being only one, and that of an exceptional kind. In some cases, as in India, the widow may only be taken by a younger brother of the deceased

[1] Robertson Smith, *Kinship and Marriage in Early Arabia*, pp. 145 sqq. London, 1903.

husband, and in this case the marriage may be a relic of polyandry ; but in most parts of the world the levirate is probably nothing more than a means of keeping the care of the children and any property belonging to the wife within the clan or family in one form or another. It is probably only very exceptionally that there is any relation between the levirate and polyandry.

CHAPTER V

FATHER-RIGHT AND MOTHER-RIGHT

CHAPTER V

FATHER-RIGHT AND MOTHER-RIGHT

I NOW come to a subject which, though not really difficult, has yet been the occasion of an extraordinary amount of misunderstanding, the subject of mother-right and father-right. These institutions are often known as the matriarchate and patriarchate respectively. But these inappropriate terms are rapidly going out of use, owing to the general recognition of the fact that there is no question of rule by women in the great majority of states to which the name matriarchate has been applied, moreover, because even in the case of the so-called patriarchate, the mode of exerting authority is not the most characteristic feature of the institution. Father-right and mother-right are more convenient and correct terms, in that they denote the determination of rights, duties, privileges, and so on, through the father and mother respectively.

I must begin by considering certain social processes which will have to be discussed in connexion with this subject. Most of the misunderstanding which surrounds it is due to the fact that processes which are entirely distinct from one another have been confused together and considered under one designation.

The first and most misunderstood of these processes is descent. This term has been used indifferently for the way in which membership of the group is determined, and for the modes of transmission of property, rank or office. As will shortly be shown, these processes do not always correspond with one another. In many cases, for instance, a man may belong to the social group of his mother, and yet receive the property or office of his father ; and it is of the utmost importance that these different social processes should be distinguished.

I will begin with *Descent*. Whenever I use this term it will apply to membership of a group, and to this only. We speak of descent as patrilineal when a child belongs to the social group of his father, and as matrilineal when he belongs to the social group of his mother. As was seen in the first chapter, social groups are of many different kinds, and it is necessary to consider to which of these groups descent will apply. The first point to note is that the use of the term is only of value when the group is unilateral. Therefore, the groups to which it applies most definitely are the clan and the moiety ; where, owing to the principle of exogamy, a child must belong to the group of the father or mother, but cannot belong to both. The use of the term has little sense, and consequently little value, in the case of the bilateral grouping, of which the *taviti* of the Solomon Islands is so good an example, for this group includes relatives on the sides of both father and mother ; the like will hold good in general of the social groups I call kindreds. In the case of the joint family, on the other hand, the term has a definite meaning, and is useful. We can distinguish between the patrilineal and matrilineal forms of the joint family, and the process by which a person comes to be a member of one or the other is a good example of descent. In the case of the simple family, in the strict sense, we might also speak of descent. Thus, our own family system might be regarded as an example of patrilineal descent, in that we take the name of the father ; though it is hardly customary to use the term in this case.

Descent can also be used of the process by which a person becomes a member of a class. In our own society, in which classes are not strictly delimited, descent of this kind is not a definite process, but the term is wholly appropriate in the case of the classes of Germany and Polynesia. In Germany, at any rate before the war, the child of a noble father was always noble, and took the prefix " *von* " ; and the same is true of Polynesian society, where the child of noble parents is always noble, though there are often complexities in the case of marriage between noble and commoner.

It is, however, when dealing with the clan or the moiety of the dual organization that descent becomes of pre-eminent importance, and in connexion with those modes of social grouping the term is indispensable.

The next process to be considered is the transmission of property, and I propose to use *Inheritance* for this process, and to confine the meaning of the term to this sense. Whenever, therefore, I speak of inheritance, it is understood that I am referring to the transmission of property.

The third process to be considered is the transmission of office, and I propose to use the term *Succession* for this process. This is not altogether satisfactory, for it conflicts to some extent with legal usage, in which the term succession applies to property. It would perhaps be more satisfactory if we could find some other word for the transmission of rank and office. The sense in which I propose to use the term, however, agrees with ordinary usage. We speak of a king as being succeeded by his son, and of a man being succeeded in his benefice or office ; and until some better term can be found I propose to use the term succession for the process of transmission of office. When a man succeeds his father, succession is patrilineal. When succession is through the mother, it will be matrilineal. It will be noticed that I have used somewhat different language in referring to the two kinds of succession. I have spoken of a man succeeding his father, but of succession through the mother. This phraseology is adopted because it is exceptional in matrilineal succession—and the same holds good of inheritance—for a person to succeed, or inherit from, his or her mother. The usual case is that he inherits from, or succeeds, his mother's brother, this being one of a number of important functions which fall to the lot of this relative in matrilineal systems.

One other feature of matrilineal inheritance and succession

must be noted.   When a man who possesses property or holds office dies, the person who inherits or succeeds is often his brother next in order of age, and only when the last surviving brother dies does the property or rank pass to the sister's child. Inheritance or succession by the brother may also accompany father-right, and when this occurs it may be regarded as a process intermediate between father-right and mother-right.

Before I leave the topics of descent, inheritance and succession I must mention a special case which introduces a complication.   When the people who follow an occupation form a group of a kind which may be called domestic, so that a person necessarily follows the occupation of the group of which he becomes a member by birth, are we to speak of the case as one of descent or succession?   The case is of no great importance, and we may regard it as one in which descent and succession cover one another.   We can speak either of descent or succession according to the special point of view from which the case is being regarded.

I can now pass to the subject of *Authority*.   In father-right the case is usually simple, authority being exerted by the father, or some other more senior relative on the male side. Even here, however, the case may be complicated by the relations between social groups of different kinds, especially the family and the clan, or perhaps more strictly between the household and the clan.

In the case of the clan, the problem of authority is far from simple, and we have at present little evidence about its nature.   It is in connexion with the family and household as groups within the clan that authority becomes of especial interest.   In the state of father-right, the father or father's father is, so far as we know, always the head of the family and household, and the matter presents no special difficulty or interest.   It is in the nature of the household in mother-right that we often find a state of affairs of much interest.   In many communities with matrilineal descent the father or father's father is definitely, so far as the clan is concerned, the head of the household, but in other cases the head of the household is the mother's brother. The household in these cases consists of the man and his brothers, his sisters and their children, but not the children of the man himself or of his brothers, who will belong to the households of their wives. In this case authority in the household is exerted by the brothers, or, looked at from the point of view of the children, by the mother's brothers. The husbands of the sisters will not form part of the household, or, if members of the household group, permanently or temporarily, are without authority, and rank in this respect behind the brothers of their wives. Similarly, the brothers or mother's brothers, who are the dispensers of authority in their own houses, will be without authority, or occupy only a subordinate position, in the households of their wives and children. This kind of organization has been termed the *Avunculate*, in order to indicate the important position occupied by the maternal uncle. In an example of such a household recorded among the Seri Indians of Lower California, the male members sat under a rude shelter in order of precedence, the eldest brother nearest the fire, his brothers next to him in order of age, and then, often outside the shelter and exposed to the rain, the husbands of the women of the household.

In exceptional cases, especially in North America, authority is exerted by the women in a very definite way. Thus, among the Iroquois and Huron, women were the heads of households, and also exerted much authority in the tribe, electing the chiefs and forming the majority of the tribal council, though the actual chiefs were men.[1] In other cases there is a definite division of authority between a woman and her brothers, the woman having the deciding voice in some matters and the brothers in others.

The last aspect of father-right and mother-right to be mentioned before I go on to consider the nature of these

---

[1] L. H. Morgan, *Ancient Society.*

states, is one with which perhaps I ought to have dealt in
the second chapter, namely, the place of residence in case of
marriage. Two kinds of marriage have been distinguished,
according as the wife goes to live with her husband, or the
husband goes to live with his wife.   These two kinds are known
as *patrilocal* and *matrilocal* respectively.   As a general rule
patrilocal marriage is associated with father-right, and
matrilocal marriage with mother-right, but the association
is far from invariable. Even when marriage is patrilocal,
the married couple often reside with the wife's people for a
time, or the wife may return to her parents' home for the
birth of her first child, this and other similar customs
suggesting the influence of ideas derived from mother-
right.

I have now described the chief features of social organization
which serve to distinguish mother- from father-right, and I
can proceed to describe some of the varied forms which these
institutions take.   It is often far from easy to decide, from
published records, the exact nature of the social practices
which have been cited under one or other of the two heads
we are considering.   This doubt is usually due to failure to
distinguish between descent, on the one hand, and inheritance
and succession on the other.   There are certainly many
societies which have been described as examples of father-right,
or of patrilineal descent, in which the conclusion that they
are so rests on observation of the succession of chieftainship,
and on failure to observe the less obvious nature of descent in
the group.   A striking example of a mistake of this kind in
Melanesia has recently been corrected by Mr. Fox.   In his book
on the Melanesians, Dr. Codrington states that in San Cristoval
and adjacent islands of the Solomons, descent follows the father.[1]
It may be noted, in passing, that this statement comes from
one who paid especial attention to social organization.   At
first he regarded the San Cristoval story as incredible, and

---

[1] *The Melanesians.*

only accepted it after repeated statements of his informant. Mr. Fox has now shown conclusively that everywhere in this region descent is matrilineal, except in the clan of the chiefs and a few other special cases, but succession to chieftainship is patrilineal. Dr. Codrington's mistake must have been due either to his failure to distinguish between descent and succession, or to his reliance on the testimony of only one witness, who, in that case, would probably have been a member of a chiefly clan.

It will, I think, be instructive if I continue to illustrate the complexity of the subject by means of Melanesia. This archipelago is usually regarded as a characteristic area of communities with mother-right. In the majority of its islands descent is matrilineal, each person belonging to the clan or moiety of his or her mother. On the other hand, succession is everywhere patrilineal. I do not know of a single case in Melanesia where a chief is succeeded by his sister's son, the characteristic form of succession in complete mother-right. When we turn to the process of inheritance we find a complicated state of affairs, from which it seems that inheritance is in an intermediate position between the matrilineal and the patrilineal modes. In most parts of this region some kinds of property pass to the children, and other kinds to the sisters' children ; while in some cases in which property passes to the children, payments have to be made to the sisters' children, which suggests that they constitute recognitions of some right of inheritance on their part.[1]

The object most frequently inherited in the female line in Melanesia is land. The study of this subject is complicated by the co-existence of communism in property, which I shall consider in the next chapter. When land is the common property of the clan, inheritance will naturally be of the same kind as descent. If descent is matrilineal, the land of the clan must necessarily also pass in that line. Moreover, wherever

[1] See *The History of Melanesian Society*, ii, chap. xix.

we know of the individual ownership of land in Melanesia, it either passes to the sisters' children, or, if the children inherit, payments similar to those of the heriot of our own culture have to be made to the sisters' children.

I have considered the mother-right of Melanesia at length, because it well illustrates the complex nature which the institution may exhibit. It is possible that this complex character is exceptional, but no example of mother-right should be accepted as simple, unless the records show clearly that the investigator has paid explicit attention to the distinction between descent, inheritance and succession.

A good example of complete mother-right is that of the Khasi of Assam. Here descent in the clan is matrilineal; the house and other property belong to the woman, and are inherited by daughters; and the chief is succeeded by his brother, or by the son of his eldest sister. The husband and father only has authority in those special cases in which, some time after his marriage, he removes his wife with her children from her house, and takes them to another house.[1]

Other complete examples of mother-right occur in Sumatra, where we find the extreme case in which the husband does not live with his wife: she dwells with her brothers, and is only occasionally visited by her husband. Descent, inheritance and succession are all matrilineal; property and rank, however, are enjoyed by the brothers before they pass to the sisters' children, a practice to which I have already referred. I must be content with these examples and must refer you to my article on Mother-right [2] for examples of the nature of the institution of mother-right in other parts of the world.

I can now pass to a problem of great interest in connexion

---

[1] P. R. Gurdon, *The Khasis*, 1907.

[2] Hastings' *Encyclopædia*; also Frazer, *Totemism and Exogamy*. I may take this opportunity to point out an error in the account of the Aztecs; in that article I ascribe to them matrilineal institutions, this opinion being based on a statement that a ruler was succeeded by his brother or his sister's son. Other and more complete records seem to show that, in general, the Aztecs were definitely a patrilineal people.

with mother-right, which will also serve incidentally to illustrate the concept of survival, and its importance in the study of social organization. I have already said that, in characteristic examples of mother-right, the mother's brother is the head of the household, and is the chief dispenser of authority over his sisters' children, a position which is perfectly natural in a society where his sisters live with him, and are only occasionally visited by their husbands. In many parts of the world, where descent, inheritance, and succession are patrilineal, it is found that authority is vested in the mother's brother equally with, or often to a greater extent than, in the father. Thus, in Torres Straits, where descent, inheritance and succession are definitely patrilineal, the mother's brother has more authority over the child than its father. A child who refuses to obey its father will at once respond to the slightest wish of its maternal uncle. Moreover, it is significant that, in the relation between uncle and nephew, property is especially important, the sister's son having the privilege, theoretically at any rate, of taking any possession of his uncle which he chooses.[1]

Similar close relations between a man and his mother's brother are found in many parts of the world. Thus, they occur in Africa, the Ba-Ronga of Delagoa Bay presenting an example of special privileges of almost exactly the same kind as those of Melanesia.[2] Similar relations between a man and his maternal uncle are frequent in North America, and, in a less degree, in India.[3] Even in Europe we have evidence of the former presence of a special relation between uncle and nephew. According to Tacitus it existed among the Germans; while the frequent mention of the sister's son in old English ballads has been held to point to the former existence of a similar custom among ourselves. Perhaps the most striking example of the relation between a man and his maternal uncle

---

[1] Cambridge, *Anth. Exp. to Torres Straits*, v, 144 seq.

[2] Junod, *The Life of a South African Tribe*, i, 253.

[3] Radin, "The Clan Organization of the Winnebago": *Amer. Anth.*, 1910.

in a patrilineal community comes from Fiji.   Here the sister's
son, called the *vasu*, not only has the right to take the property
of his mother's brother, but, if his mother's brother is a chief,
he can help himself to the property, including the wives, of
any of his uncle's subjects.

Those patrilineal societies in which the mother's brother
has special authority over, or other close social relations
with, his sister's son, are often situated near other societies
organized on a matrilineal basis.   Thus, in Fiji, the special
position of the *vasu*, or sister's son, is characteristic of the
patrilineal island of Viti Levu, while the adjacent island of
Vanua Levu has a matrilineal society of the dual kind.   Elsewhere the patrilineal societies where the mother's brother has
a privileged position are, as a rule, not far removed from
other societies of a matrilineal kind.

Since the relations between a man and his mother's brother
are such as would follow naturally from a state of mother-
right, it has been concluded that, where the relation is found
in a patrilineal society, it is a relic or survival of an antecedent
state of mother-right.

Other features characteristic of mother-right also occur
occasionally in patrilineal societies, and have similarly been
regarded as survivals of earlier matrilineal institutions.
Thus, where a person belongs to his or her mother's clan,
children of the same mother cannot marry, for they will be
members of the same group.   There will, however, be no such
bar in a matrilineal society to the marriage of children of
one father and different mothers, for, if the wives of the father
come from different clans, the children would necessarily belong
to those clans.   The marriage of half-brother and sister,
which was allowed in Athens, has, therefore, been regarded
as a survival of mother-right, for, in this case, it was only
between children of one father, but different mothers, that
such a marriage was permitted.

An indication of an early state of mother-right has also
been found in the traditions of descent from a woman frequently

possessed by societies which are now patrilineal. Still another trace of an early mother-right has been seen in the theme of unwitting patricide so prominent in early literature, for it is where descent is matrilineal that the father is especially likely to be unknown to his children.

A good example of a social custom of another kind which points to an antecedent state of mother-right occurs in the island of Ambrim in the New Hebrides, the present organization of which is strictly patrilineal. According to the tradition of its inhabitants, certain religious ceremonies of this island have been introduced from without, while others are believed to be indigenous. In some of the latter class of ceremony the leading participants have, at one stage of the proceedings, to visit their mothers' villages, while no such feature accompanies the rites of more recent introduction. On either side of Ambrim lie islands which present characteristic examples of mother-right. Here, ceremonies in which a person is concerned would naturally take place in his mother's village ; and the fact that, in adjoining patrilineal islands, visits to the mother's village should form part of the ritual of ancient ceremonies, while this feature is absent from ceremonies of more recent introduction, is a strong indication that the present state of father-right has been preceded by matrilineal institutions such as still exist in neighbouring islands.[1]

It is a characteristic of the English school of ethnology that, following the example of E. B. Tylor, it has always attached great importance to such survivals as a means of tracing the development of human institutions, and the presence of a large accumulation of such facts as I have just recorded has led English students to the generalization that mother-right was the original state of human society, and that, where existing human societies are patrilineal, their father-right has been preceded by earlier institutions on a matrilineal basis. The importance of survivals, however, is not accepted by many students on the Continent, and by some in our own

---

[1] *Journ. Roy. Anth. Inst.*, xlv, 1915, 229 et seq.

country ; while evidence of this kind is almost entirely dis-
regarded by American ethnologists ; and in recent years
the belief in the universality of mother-right, which had become
a dogma in this country, has been seriously called in question.

The problem is closely bound up with another of great
importance and interest, to which I have so far made no
reference. All students of human culture who believed
in the universal priority of mother-right also held another
belief, which, when I first began the study of ethnology,
had become an unquestioned dogma in this country. It was
held that the societies of widely separated parts of the world,
such as Europe, Australia, and America, had evolved
independently of one another, features of culture common to
them having been due to certain supposed similarities in the
activity of the human mind. It was postulated, for instance,
in the case now being discussed, that certain conditions of
early human society, such as the certainty of the physiological
fact of motherhood and the uncertainty of fatherhood, had
everywhere produced a state in which a man belonged to the
group of his mother, whose relation to himself was known,
rather than to the group of his father, who might be altogether
unknown, and was, in any case, uncertain. A great stimulus
was given to this view early in this century by the discovery
that there are people, such as the Australian aboriginals,
who are unaware of the relation between procreation and
conception. It was assumed that this and the other factors
which had produced matrilineal institutions had been in
universal operation at one stage of the progress of human
society, and that knowledge of the physiological nature of
fatherhood had produced the social recognition of the father
and the development of social groups in which the relation
between father and child was the central feature.

About ten years ago it began to be recognized in this country
—it had already been recognized elsewhere—that the view,
that human society had undergone this independent development on similar lines in different parts of the world, was far

too simple.   It was recognized, at any rate by many students, and the number is rapidly growing, that the existing institutions of mankind are not the result of a simple process of evolution, but that there has been in action a highly complicated process of blending and interaction of cultures, often widely different from one another, the outcome of the interaction being complex structures, not only containing elements derived from both the blended cultures, but also new products of the interaction. The mother-right of Melanesia, with its mixture of matrilineal descent and patrilineal succession, its inheritance of some kinds of property in the male line, and of others in the female line, is a good example of such a complex product of mixture. It was, as a matter of fact, one of the features of Melanesian society which first led me to recognize the inadequacy of the view with which until then I had been content.   There is abundant evidence that the present state of Melanesian society has come about through a process in which an earlier matrilineal society suffered great modification at the hands of immigrant people imbued with patrilineal sentiments.   These immigrants, being adopted as chiefs, were able to hand on their rank to their children, and thus to institute patrilineal succession ; but were powerless in many cases to alter descent, and were only able to influence inheritance where the objects concerned were those which they had themselves introduced.[1] In the case of Melanesia there seems to be no reason to give up the view that, where patrilineal institutions exist, they have been superposed upon an older matrilineal society.   If, however, social institutions thus arise as a product of the interaction of different cultures, we are no longer justified in believing that change has always been in one direction.   It becomes possible that matrilineal immigrants or conquerors may in some cases impose their social practices on a patrilineal

---

[1] [It is possible that Rivers is not quite correct in this instance. The superposition of the chiefly class probably took place elsewhere, and the resulting complex form of society was transferred bodily to various parts of the earth.   This point, however, does not affect his main contentions.]

people, and it is probable that such a process has taken place in certain societies.

Thus, in North America, those who believe in the universal priority of matrilineal institutions have to reckon with the fact that the two most advanced societies of North America (excluding Mexico as part of Central America), namely, the Iroquois and the Pueblo Indians, were conspicuous examples of mother-right. It is, of course, possible that these societies may be examples of a primitive state which has survived in these advanced communities, while elsewhere the change to father-right has been accompanied by degeneration ; but no one has put forward this uncomfortable doctrine,[1] and it is noteworthy that a leading advocate of the universal priority of mother-right in this country, Mr. Sidney Hartland, evades the difficulty by not mentioning its existence.

At the same time I should like to urge that giving up the doctrine of the universal priority of mother-right does not involve the acceptance of the priority of father-right, which, through the influence of Sir Henry Maine, is still, I believe, current in writings on the history of political institutions. This view is even more untenable than that which I have just been combating.

The conclusion to which those students whose views are based on a wide comparative study are now coming, is that we cannot regard the early state of human society as one in which it is possible to speak either of father-right or mother-right. If the reader accepts the scheme of the history of marriage, and of the family and clan, which I sketched in the last chapter, it will no longer be possible to hold that either father-right or mother-right characterized the earliest forms of human society. If I am right in supposing that, in the collecting stage, man went about the world in small

---

[1] [This " uncomfortable doctrine" is advanced by Perry in *The Children of the Sun*, chap. xvi. Rivers was the first to note the fact he adduces ; and the prosecution of the line of thought first trod by him in this matter leads to illuminating results.]

loosely defined bands, the social processes we call descent, inheritance and succession would be of a vague indefinite kind, and might, in many cases, hardly be said to exist at all. If the consequent growth of the groups in size [1] led to the formation of clans, it becomes possible that the evolution may have taken place in two directions, producing patrilineal and matrilineal institutions respectively.   In some cases the loose band may have evolved into a patrilineal clan without any intermediate stage of mother-right.   According to American ethnologists, this is what has actually happened in their continent, while, rightly or wrongly, they also believe that, in some cases, highly organized matrilineal peoples have imposed their rules upon ruder patrilineal peoples. The situation is one for an open mind.   We should wait further evidence, and treat every region on its own merits, avoiding such generalizations as that of the universal priority of matrilineal institutions until intensive work in each area has shown us the nature of the process by which its social institutions have come to be what they are.

[1] [Due to the discovery of agriculture.]

CHAPTER VI

PROPERTY

CHAPTER VI

PROPERTY

WHEN discussing the functions of the family and clan it was found that property could be held in different ways according to its nature and origin. In this chapter I propose to deal with the subject explicitly. The main problem with which I shall deal is how far in different human societies property is held by social groups, and how far it belongs to the individual. I shall also inquire into the nature of the group in which common ownership is vested when it is present.

We shall find that the matter is far from simple, and that in many societies where the institution of individual property is definite, there are nevertheless customs which show the existence of a group-interest in property at variance with individual rights. I may begin by going briefly through the different kinds of social group that have been considered, and state briefly how they stand in relation to individualism and communism in respect of property.

We may lay it down as a definite proposition, that wherever we find the family (in the narrow sense) as the dominant feature of the social organization it is combined with the institution of individual property. The exact nature of ownership may differ, and variations such as those characterizing Primogeniture, Junior Right, or Borough English, and other forms of inheritance may be found, but in all cases in which society is founded mainly or altogether on the family, property is owned by individuals. The community has certain claims on these individual rights in the form of taxation, etc., but the prominent feature from the broad comparative point of view is the individual character of ownership.

Taking the various Indian forms of the joint family as instances of this form of social grouping, we find in most cases common ownership is a prominent feature. Thus, in the joint family of Bengal, property is altogether in common, while in the *mitakshara* system of other parts of India only ancestral property is thus held in common, every member of the group having full rights over property acquired by his own exertions. Property is regarded as ancestral when it has been transmitted for two generations, and it is then regarded as inalienable. In the matrilineal joint family of Malabar property is held in common, being controlled by the senior male member of the group. In all these forms of the joint family we have a definite departure from individual ownership in the direction of communal ownership, the special feature of the communism being that common ownership is limited to a relatively small group bound together by close ties of genealogical relationship or kinship.

If now we pass to the bilateral group of the kindred, we find again this feature of communal ownership. There is evidence that in the kindreds of Northern Europe property was to a large extent in common,[1] and this is certainly the case in the modern example I have already cited more than once, the *taviti* of Eddystone Island in the Solomons. In this mode of social grouping land and other forms of property are held in common by the *taviti*, and where a person has individual rights in his land or other property these are subject to many claims on the part of other members of his *taviti*. I will not describe the nature of these claims here, because they are essentially of the same kind as those found in association with the clan-organization, and can best be exemplified in connexion with that form of social organization, to which I can now pass.

The study of the relation of the clan to property is complicated by the feature, which we have seen to produce

---

[1] Philpotts, *Kindred and Clan*.

complications of other kinds, that the clan-grouping is always, so far as we know, complicated by the co-existence of a family grouping of some kind. Thus, in Melanesia, where our information is more exact than in other parts of the world, not only is the family in the limited sense recognized, but there are still more definitely present examples, in one form or another, of the joint-family. Thus, in the island of Ambrim, where I was able to obtain a detailed account of the regulations concerning ownership, it was clear that the most important social group in relation to property was one called *vantinbül*. There was some doubt about the exact limits of this group, but it was certainly a kinship group consisting in the main of persons genealogically related in the male line, though it also included the daughters of members and their children, membership of the *vantinbül* in the female line then lapsing. In other parts of Melanesia the groups in which ownership is vested are kinship groups of this kind rather than moieties or clans. Thus, in Pentecost Island, which is the seat of the dual organization, the group which held property in common was the one called *verana*, which, so far as I could discover in a far too brief investigation, was a kinship group similar to the *vantinbul* of Ambrim.

I have given an account of the Ambrim mode of grouping because I do not think I can better illustrate the nature of the subject than by taking this island as an example of the ownership of a simple society. I will begin with the ownership of land. Here land was in one sense held to be the property of the clan. People of any *vantinbul* might clear patches in the uncultivated land, which would in time become the property of the *vantinbül* of the clearer. If a *vantinbul* died out, its land became the property of the village as a whole ; it went out of cultivation and then shared the complete indifference of the people to the ownership of uncultivated land.

It was evident that in Ambrim there was no appearance even of the individual ownership of land. It was the custom in this island to indicate the nature of the ownership of an object by

means of the possessive pronoun.   Where there was individual
ownership a man would indicate the fact by the use of the
personal pronoun, and would speak of " my bow and arrow "
or " my armlet ", but, with one unimportant exception, he
would never speak of " my land ", and would always say " our
land ".   Moreover, this mode of speech was no empty form.
A man might clear a piece of ground entirely by his own labour,
and might plant and tend it without help from anyone, but
any member of his *vantinbül* could nevertheless help himself
to any of its produce without asking leave or informing the
cultivator.   Inhabitants of the village belonging to a *vantinbul*
other than that of the cultivator might also take produce,
but had to ask leave.   Since such permission, however, was
never refused, the communism extended in practice to the
whole clan.   For property of other kinds the case differed
with the kind of object.   The most frequent and important
fact determining the nature of ownership in Ambrim is
whether the object is indigenous or introduced, indigenous
objects being owned by the *vantinbül* or other larger group,
while introduced objects may be owned by individuals.   A good
example of the difference is presented by the weapons of
Ambrim, of which there are four : the spear, club, bow and
arrow, and sling.   The first two are common property, and a
man will always say " our spear " and " our club ", but, on the
other hand, the bow and arrow and sling are individually
owned objects, and people said " my bow and arrow " and
" my sling ".   Associated with this usage was a definite
tradition that the people had always had the spear and club,
while the sling and bow and arrow had been introduced from
a neighbouring island.

There was some reason to suppose that another factor which
had influenced ownership was whether an object had been made
by individual or common labour.   Thus one of the objects of
Melanesian culture which is usually, if not always, the subject
of common ownership is the canoe, and at one time I had the
impression that this was because it was made by the common

labour of the community. It is highly doubtful whether this is the real explanation, whether it is not rather the result of rationalization of tradition, which must always be borne in mind as a possibility in the case of rude, or indeed of any explanation of social customs or institutions. For one of the objects most constantly made by communal effort in Melanesia is the house, and yet this is usually certainly in Ambrim, an individual possession, or at least the possession of the family in the limited sense.

Such facts as those, however, fail to reveal the great extent to which communistic sentiments concerning property dominate the people of Melanesia. One who lives among Melanesians is continually impressed by little occurrences which indicate the strength and pervasiveness of these sentiments. I must be content with one example. When in the Banks Islands, a small group north of the New Hebrides, I worked out the history of a plot of land which was cleared about four generations ago. The greater part of the plot had been divided up between the children of the clearer, and had since been regarded as the individual property of their descendants, but part of the original plot had been left for the common use of all the descendants of the original clearer. I was told that disputes were frequent concerning the portions of the land which were owned individually, while there were never any quarrels concerning the part which had been left for the common use of all.

In one part of Melanesia, in Fiji, which differs from the rest in the greater definiteness of its chieftainship, and in several other respects, probably as the result of Polynesian influence, the communism is still more definite. Thus, there is a custom called *kerekere*, whereby persons may take the property of others, to such an extent that it has served as an effectual bar to the adoption of European methods of trading. A Fijian who sets up as a trader is liable to have his goods appropriated by anyone who comes into his store, to such an extent as to make his success impossible.

About the Polynesian Islands of the Pacific our information is less definite, but here again it would seem that communism exists in a pronounced form. I must be content to give you an example from my own experience. I was travelling on a boat with four inhabitants of Niue or Savage Island, and took the opportunity of inquiring into their social organization. At the end of the sitting they said they would like now to examine me about my customs, and, using my own concrete methods, one of the first questions was directed to discover what I should do with a sovereign if I earned one. In response to my somewhat lame answers, they asked me point-blank whether I should share it with my parents and brothers and sisters. When I replied that I would not usually, and certainly not necessarily do so, and that it was not our general custom, they found my reply so amusing that it was long before they left off laughing. Their attitude towards my individualism was of exactly the same order as that which we adopt towards such a custom as the couvade, in which the man goes to bed when his wife has a child, and revealed the presence of a communistic sentiment of a deeply seated kind.

The ownership of property in Oceania has other points of interest, to which I shall return after sketching very briefly the state of affairs in other parts of the world.

The land-tenure of Africa differs from that of Melanesia in a very striking respect. In Melanesia chiefs have no functions in relation to land. If they possess land they own it in the same way, and subject to the same communal usages, as other persons, and, in one case at least, they are not even landowners, and only obtain land for their gardens by the grace of their subjects. Among the Bantu of Africa, on the other hand, the position of chiefs in this respect is very different. They hold the land and distribute it among their subjects, but they probably only act in this respect as the representatives of the people as a whole ; for the Ba-Ila have a rule that the chief may only sell land after obtaining the permission of his people. In this case, and probably elsewhere among the Bantu, the chief seems to be the distributor of individual rights to the use of land rather than its owner.

According to the available accounts, land assigned by a Ba-Ila chief to one of his subjects is regarded as the assignee's individual property, but this individual ownership is subject to the restriction that any of his elder relatives on both sides have the right to take what they want. We have thus a form of common ownership, or rather common usufruct, which is similar to that of Melanesia in that the group concerned is a kinship-group, but there is the important difference that the right is limited to the members of the group senior to the owner. This rule also applies to other kinds of property, and Smith and Dale record how a Ba-Ila who has gained large sums by his industry in working for European settlers may be deprived of them all by his elder relatives.

As in Melanesia it would seem that the right of the elders, which is perhaps derived from a more extensive communism, is a privilege belonging to a kinship-group rather than to the clan.

In a recent paper Dundas gives an instructive case of pure individual ownership among a Bantu people. This occurs among the Wakarra, a tribe living on an island every acre of which is cultivated. Every piece of land is privately owned, and Dundas supposes that individual tenure has evolved owing to the high value which land possesses. This tribe is also exceptional in Africa, in that an owner may sell his land, but only after consulting his kinsmen in order to give them the first option. This right of the kin is of interest in relation to the common rights of kinship-groups elsewhere among the Bantu.

Dundas also records an interesting case among the Akikuyu. They have acquired their land from the earlier inhabitants. All the land thus bought by a man is held as the common property of his descendants. The senior member of the existing group of descendants is regarded as the owner, but only as representative of the group. Land is never sold, and Dundas

says that the Akikuyu cannot comprehend the sale of land,
by which I suppose he means that the sale of land is so foreign
to their sentiments that they can hardly conceive what is
meant when the idea of a sale is broached.

In West Africa there appear to be variations in different
regions, the differences probably depending on the degree of
influence of the peoples of higher culture who have for a long
time been passing into the country from the north. Thus, in
the northern parts of the region of the Gold Coast, individual
property is, according to Cardinall, as definite an institution
as among ourselves. On the coast itself, on the other hand,
the land is regarded as the property of the tribe, but any
member of the community is at liberty to clear and farm any
portion of the untilled bush. The cleared part is regarded as
his property so long as he cultivates it, and his right to it is
still recognized if he should leave it untilled for a time in
order that it may recover its fertility. In the intermediate
region, farther inland, the individual retains rights in the
trees growing on land which he has cleared but has then again
allowed to fall into disuse, thus presenting a further step towards
individual ownership.

Here, as in Melanesia, the chief has no special powers in
connexion with the land. As he has command over a larger
number of labourers, he is able to cultivate more land than the
rest, but otherwise he is no better off than any of his subjects.
There is a native saying, " Chiefs command people, not the
land." While the chiefs are thus devoid of special privileges
in relation to the land, there is an official called the *tindana*,
who has powers resting upon the tradition that he is the
representative of the original owners of the soil, whose powers
have persisted when people from elsewhere became the chiefs.
The *tindana* assigns land to new settlers, and he is called upon
to intercede with the local deity if, for any reason, such as the
spilling of blood or other crime, the land has been polluted and
there is the danger of its ceasing to yield its fruits. The
tindana is, in fact, a priest, and receives for his services a

basket of corn or other payment, which seems to correspond closely with the tithe of our own culture.

In North America there are many intermediate states between individual and communal ownership, but, as in Melanesia, where there is common ownership this seems to be vested in some form of the joint family, i.e. in a kinship-group rather than in the clan.

The case which has been supposed to point most definitely to ownership by the clan is that of the Aztecs of Mexico, where, according to some authorities, the group called *calpulli*, which is usually supposed to have been a clan, though its exact nature is doubtful, seems to have held land in common. But the constitution of the *calpulli* is doubtful, and there is reason to believe that it was a kinship-group of some kind rather than a clan. Whatever the exact nature of the tenure may have been, however, it seems certain that it had one feature which distinguished it markedly from the land-tenure of Melanesia and, at the same time, caused it to resemble the early tenures of Europe. The land of the *calpulli* was parcelled out among the male members of the group, each of whom had to cultivate his allotment, and if anyone failed in this duty the land was reallotted at the end of two years and assigned to other members of the *calpulli*. We have here a state intermediate between communal property and individual possession closely comparable with that of our own history.

The ownership of other kinds of property in North America seems to have been individual rather than communal, though we have singularly little information on the point. Superficially there is little question that individual ownership is definite, but it is a question whether here, as in other parts of the world, more detailed investigation would not show the existence of rights of other members of the group to objects which are said to be the individual property of some member of the group. Dr. Paul Radin has given me an interesting example pointing in this direction. When buying an ancient pipe from a member of the Winnebago tribe he found that a reluctance to sell was due to the sentiment of the rest of the group, in this case the joint-family.   It was acknowledged by all that the pipe was the property of the vendor, and that he had a complete right to sell it, but the whole group was animated by a sentiment towards the object which was acting as a definite bar to alienation.   It is possible that in this case the sentiment was no more than would exist in such a case among ourselves. Thus, to take a recent instance, the intention of the Duke of Westminster to sell Gainsborough's " Blue Boy " might be hindered by the existence among the Grosvenor family of a sentiment against the sale, and in some cases the sentiment might prove an effectual bar to alienation.   In the case of our own society such rights have become the subject of definite social regulations, which make up what we call law.   Where law is only customary, and has not been fixed in definite form by means of writing, there must always be an element of doubt as to whether a given act is definitely illegal or only an offence against a sentiment of the society, and Dr. Radin's case seems to be open to doubt of this kind.

I should like here to consider briefly a widespread case of ownership which has aroused much interest.   I refer to the custom by which a person may own trees growing on land which belongs to another.   This custom is frequent, for instance, in Melanesia.   Thus, in Eddystone Island a person is allowed to plant a tree on the land of another, and this is regarded as the property of himself and his descendants.   In other cases the separate ownership depends upon different laws of inheritance : while land on which trees are planted passes, according to ancient custom, to the children of the sister, the trees which a man has planted on this land may be inherited by his own children ; and it seems clear that this forms a social mechanism by which the separate ownership of trees and land has come about.   I believe that these customs in general are the result of the blending of peoples, patrilineal immigrants having succeeded in transmitting their trees to their children, while the land itself has to follow the laws of matrilineal inheritance of the indigenous inhabitants.

According to another Melanesian custom, an individual may obtain the sole right to use the fruit of certain trees by means of religious ceremonial. Thus, in the island of Ambrim in the New Hebrides, certain trees are assigned to individuals as part of the rites by which men rise from rank to rank of a graded organization called the *Mangge*, which plays a great part in the social organization of the people, and trees may also be appropriated to individual use by means of taboo marks, theft of the protected fruit being believed to bring sickness on the offender through the action of ancestral ghosts. Similarly, in Eddystone Island in the Solomons, the fruit of certain trees may only be used by an individual who pays one with the necessary powers to impose a taboo, infringement of the taboo being believed, as in Ambrim, to bring disease upon the thief. The nature of the trees thus protected suggests that they may have been introduced by immigrants who utilized religious beliefs, also introduced by them, to confine usufruct and ownership to themselves and their descendants. When I suggested this mode of origin of the practice at a meeting at which several African ethnographers were present, it was objected that such a mechanism could not apply to the separate ownership of trees in Africa, but I note a significant passage in Cardinall's account of the Gold Coast, which suggests that my explanation may also hold good there, at any rate in some cases. Cardinall notes that in one district certain trees, including the locust-bean, are owned by the chiefs. There is clear evidence that the chiefs are descendants of immigrants, and Cardinall expressly notes that the locust-bean is not indigenous to the country. He believes that the right of the chiefs was obtained from the *tindana*, but the foreign origin of the locust-bean suggests that its ownership by the chiefs may have had an origin similar to that to which I have referred the similar custom of Melanesia.

The general conclusion which can be drawn from the foregoing account is that both in Melanesia and Africa there is much evidence for an early state of communal ownership of land and of certain kinds of property, while in Melanesia there is reason to believe that individual ownership has come about as the result of influence from without. On the other hand, in those cases in which we have the most definite evidence of communal ownership, the group concerned is not the clan but a group within the clan or moiety, which consists of kin, of persons related to one another by kinship and not by sibship. Behind the definite regulations concerning ownership by these smaller groups there is often the tradition of ownership by the clan, and it seems probable that there was at one time common ownership by the clan or moiety which has been replaced, at any rate in practice, by ownership in which the common rights rest on kinship.

I have dealt in this chapter especially with the topics of communal and individual ownership, and I may now consider briefly whether the distinction between the two kinds of ownership can be correlated with different modes of inheritance. The problem is important, because if communal ownership was associated with the clan-organization, and if, as we have reason to believe, there is an association between this form of organization and mother-right, we should expect to find a correlation between communal ownership and inheritance by the sister's children, rather than by the own children. Here, as in general, we are hampered by the paucity of evidence. In Melanesia the information given by Codrington would lead us definitely to the view that communal ownership and inheritance by the sister's children run together. On the other hand, Codrington's work was almost entirely confined to the matrilineal regions of Melanesia, and my own work has shown the existence of communal ownership of the most definite kind in two purely patrilineal societies. Nevertheless, there are facts pointing definitely to the close connexion between communal ownership and mother-right, on the one hand, and individual ownership and father-right on the other hand. Thus, it is significant that trees which, as we have seen, are owned individually, are in general inherited by the children, while the land on which they grow passes to the sister's children. Again, such organizations as the *Mangge* of Ambrim, through the agency of which men attain the individual ownership of trees, are certainly due to a patrilineal society which has been imposed upon an older matrilineal basis. While the evidence cannot be regarded as conclusive, there is much evidence from Melanesia of the association of communal ownership with mother-right.

When we turn to Africa, on the other hand, evidence bearing on this problem is almost wholly lacking. Thus, Cardinall, who has given us the most explicit and complete account of land-tenure which we possess from any African Society, gives us no information whatever of the nature of descent, and none of those details of inheritance and ownership which so often enable us to infer the nature of earlier forms of social organization. His evidence makes it clear that communal ownership goes back to an early state of society of which the *tindana* is a survival, but we have no evidence by which we can infer of what kind this early society was.

I cannot leave the subject of communal ownership without a brief reference to its association with sexual communism. Here again our most satisfactory evidence comes from Melanesia, where there is a fairly definite association of the two kinds of communism. In several parts of Melanesia there is definite evidence for the association of communal ownership with customs which point to the existence in the past of organized sexual communism, which is still present here and there in Melanesia. The association is not, however, invariable. In Eddystone Island, which presents one of the most definite examples of communal ownership, the practice of monogamy exists in a degree which puts it far above that of our own society, but it may be noted that the very strict limitation of sexual relations only occurs after marriage, and that before marriage there is a state of organized communism which may be the survival of an earlier state in which this communism also existed after marriage.

I have in this chapter confined my attention almost exclusively to the topics of individual and communal ownership and the influence upon inheritance of the states of father- and mother-right. I may conclude by giving a few examples from rude peoples of customs which exist or have existed among ourselves. Thus, in Melanesia there are customs which resemble that known among ourselves as heriot. When, in some parts of Melanesia, the owner of a tree growing upon the land of another dies, the heir has to make a payment to the owner of the land, or, when property passes to the son of an owner, a similar payment is made by the heir to the sister's children of the deceased.

Again, the custom of junior right, in which the youngest son is the chief heir, of which our own custom of Borough English is an example, exists in many rude societies. In some cases it has a feature which suggests the origin of the practice. It is sometimes the rule that the youngest son inherits the house, while other kinds of property pass to his eldest brothers, or are shared by all. This practice seems to be the result of the custom by which the sons, as they marry, set up establishments of their own, so that, when the father dies, only the youngest son is still living at home.

Problems of especial interest arise again in connexion with primogeniture. In Melanesia certainly, and probably in other parts of the world, while the eldest son has no special rights in relation to inheritance, he is the subject of special ceremonial which does not take place in the case of later children. There is reason to believe that in some parts of the world these customs may be connected with the belief in reincarnation—the belief that the ghost of the father, or more frequently of the father's father, is reincarnated in the eldest child—and that this belief accounts for the special treatment. The belief in such reincarnation has a wide distribution, and it therefore becomes possible that the privileged position of the eldest child in other societies, possibly even in our own, in relation to property, may be connected with a similar belief. In India, however, the evidence is against any connexion between primogeniture and reincarnation : it is not necessarily the eldest son whom the ghost of the grandfather inhabits, but any son who is born soon after the death of the grandfather.

CHAPTER VII

FRATERNITIES AND SECRET SOCIETIES

CHAPTER VII

FRATERNITIES AND SECRET SOCIETIES

I CAN now pass to a form of grouping very different in nature from those which I have so far been considering. The reader will remember that one mode of classification of social groups suggested in the first chapter depends on whether the association is voluntary or involuntary, whether the individual becomes a member of a group by such a process as the act of birth, or whether he joins it voluntarily. With one or two exceptions, such as the occupations entered by apprenticeship or initiation, all the groups so far considered have been of the involuntary kind; and I propose now to consider a mode of grouping in which the association is voluntary. In some cases these groups are entered during childhood, the parents or other relatives acting as sponsors, but this only modifies to some extent their voluntary character.

The groups I have now to consider are usually known as secret societies. This term is unfortunate, for, in several parts of the world, notably in Melanesia and Africa, organizations occur which are shown by their whole structure and function to be closely allied to one another, and yet in one place the proceedings may be kept wholly secret, while in another much of the ritual is open to all. Moreover, it is probable that associations characterized by the secrecy of their proceedings are of several different kinds, and that the feature of secrecy does not provide a satisfactory means of classification.

A more important feature, which seems to be common to all, is that the associations now to be considered are entered by a process of initiation, though here again the associations which are joined by a process of initiation include groups of several different kinds.

Moreover, a process of initiation, similar to that by which members are submitted to organizations, is a frequent feature of admission to certain occupations, especially to that of priest or shaman, and in some cases there are close points of similarity even in detail between the two kinds of initiation. This sharing of the feature of initiation is a valuable guide to the relation of different forms of grouping to one another, but initiation itself can hardly be utilized as a means of defining the associations now to be considered.

A feature of great importance in connexion with these associations is their relation to sex-differentiation. In a large number of cases, membership of the associations in question is limited to persons of one sex, and especially the male sex, and they might therefore be called sex-associations. Similar associations are found occasionally which are limited to women, but often these are only imitations of the male organizations. Their occurrence, however, would not conflict with the view that these societies are sex-associations. Such conflict arises definitely, however, in North America, and to a less extent in Africa, where there are often associations similar in structure and function to the sex-associations to which, nevertheless, women are freely admitted. However, it is probable that in this sex-differentiation we have an important feature of the associations, and in considering their nature it would be profitable to begin with an example where this sex-differentiation is present. In giving a general account of these modes of grouping, I shall have especially in mind the societies of Melanesia.[1]

---

[1] Cf. H. Schurz, *Altersklassen und Männerbunde*, Berlin, 1902 ; H. Webster, *Primitive Secret Societies* ; Rivers, *History of Melanesian Society*, chaps. iii -v, xxiv.

Where membership of the group is limited to male persons, it is natural to find that the associations are closely connected with the institution of the men's house, that is, a house common to men, in which the men of the community, or the initiated men, dwell, eat and sleep. While it is a general feature that all the men should eat together in the men's house, there are differences with regard to sleeping. In some cases all the men sleep in the common-house, while more frequently only the bachelors sleep there, the married men sleeping in their own houses with their wives and families. It must be noticed, however, that the men's house is found in many places where there is at present no evidence for the existence of definite associations.

A feature which is frequent, but not universal, is that the association forms a hierarchy ; the members differ in status and gradually rise in rank. The group thus forms a graded body, in which each grade is entered by a process of initiation resembling that by which the association itself is entered. As a rule the process of initiation becomes more lengthy and complex the higher the rank attained. When the association is thus graded in rank it is often the rule that only those of the same rank may eat together. In such cases the common-house is divided into compartments, one to each rank, and a man is not allowed to enter a compartment belonging to a rank higher than his own.

In the New Hebrides the practice that only men of one rank may eat together is definitely connected with the fire. Each grade has its own fire, and the essential rule is that a man may only eat food cooked at a fire of his rank, at which no other food may be cooked. This feature has been only recorded with certainty in the New Hebrides, but it is probably an essential feature of all the graded societies of Melanesia. The place thus taken by fire in the rules of the organization almost certainly has a religious character, and this is quite certain in the case of the next feature of the societies, that according to which the whole organization is connected with a cult of ancestral ghosts. Many features of the ritual of initiation depend on the belief that, at this time, the initiate and the group as a whole come into relation with the ghosts of dead ancestors.[1]

Thus, in the island of Ambrim in the New Hebrides, an image is made as part of the ceremony of initiation into several of the higher ranks, and it is believed that the ghost of the grandfather of the initiate enters this image in order to watch over the career of his descendant. In another part of Melanesia, the Banks Islands, there are special societies distinguished from, though related to, the graded organization, which are called ghost societies, and are connected with ancestral ghosts.

Certain widespread features of secret associations, which have attracted much attention, are definitely connected with cults of ghosts. The masks, which form prominent objects in our museums, are, in many cases, intended to represent ghosts. In Melanesia these masks are worn especially when the members leave their secret place of meeting, and serve to keep up the general belief of the community that the organization embodies a cult of ghosts. The masks serve as one of the means by which the secrecy of the proceedings is secured. Another means to this end is the production of certain mysterious sounds, of which that produced by swinging a bull-roarer is the most widespread. This and other sounds are believed by the uninitiated to be the voices of the ghosts. In Melanesia hats take a prominent part in the ritual of the secret societies. The relation of these hats to masks is doubtful, but it is probable that the hat is only a special form of mask, and that the emphasis of that part of the mask which covers the head is connected with the sanctity of that part of the body.

Closely connected with the belief that the members of the societies are ghosts, is the frequent occurrence, in the ritual of initiation, of features which point to this process as being

---

[1] [Cf. Perry, *The Origin of Magic and Religion*, chap. vii, for the explanation of the connexion between Secret Societies and the cult of the dead.]

symbolic of death and rebirth. Thus, in Melanesia, a candidate, who leaves his family in order to be initiated, is mourned for as if he were dead, and there are frequent features of the ritual which point to its being in a large measure a symbolization of death.[1]

A feature which may be mentioned here, is that there is not infrequently a connexion between the groups, or ranks of a group, and animals or plants, which suggests some kind of relationship with totemism.

In addition to the features which bring these associations definitely into the category of religious groupings, there may be other features of a political or religious kind. Thus, wherever these organizations are found in Melanesia, there is nothing which can properly be called chieftainship, the place of the chiefs being taken by men of high rank in the organization. Or, these men of high rank may be regarded as chiefs, in which case the rank of chief is not hereditary, but is attained by a process of successive initiations. Since men only attain this rank by a lengthy process, the rulers are necessarily old men, thus producing the mode of government which has been called a gerontocracy. In Melanesia, at any rate, there is a close association between this form of government and the existence of graded organizations entered by initiation.

The economical significance of these organizations arises chiefly out of the complex system of payments which accompany initiation. When a man attains a new rank he has to make extensive payments in the form of pigs, shell-money, mats or other objects, which go partly to the man who acts as his sponsor, partly to the members of the grade of which he becomes a member. On the other hand, the men who receive these payments may be themselves candidates, or are preparing to be candidates, for a still higher rank; and the whole organization thus forms a highly complicated meshwork of

---

[1] [See Perry, *The Origin of Magic and Religion*, chap. vii.]

incomings and outgoings which involve vested interests of a
very varied kind. One of the motives for expending wealth
in order to acquire higher rank, is that the new possessor of
this higher rank will receive the payments of others who are
initiated later.

I may take this opportunity to say that, in those parts of
Melanesia where graded organizations and ghost societies
are found, the chief, almost the only, function of the objects
which are usually called money is in connexion with these
associations. The Melanesian object which corresponds most
closely with our money consists of chains of discs made from
shells. The use of definite units of length, and of multiples
of these units, bring this object into so close a resemblance
with our concept of money that it has universally received
this designation among those who have written about
Melanesia. It must be remembered, however, that in those
parts of Melanesia which possess graded organizations, this
money is used almost exclusively in connexion with the proceedings of these associations, and takes a very small place in
such transactions as the acquisition of food or the passing of
manufactured articles either from member to member of a
community, or from one community to another.

Since the groups in connexion with which the so-called
money is used are to a large extent religious associations,
the use of money is brought into close relation with religion,
and it is noteworthy that, in other parts of Melanesia, including
some where the associations are absent or of relatively small
importance, both shell-money and money of other kinds are
denoted by words, such as *tambu* and *rongo*, which mean
sacred.

Another economic function of the organizations, at any rate
in the Banks Islands, is that they form the means by which
the right to individual property is acquired. In these islands
the graded organizations co-exist with the dual organization,
with its communistic features described in an earlier chapter,
but the organizations act in a kind of opposition to these

communistic practices, each grade, or, if individual societies, each society, having a badge by means of which property is protected from all except other members of the grade or society.

The organizations thus act as a means whereby the right to individual property is maintained in an otherwise communistic society. In the New Hebrides, also, ceremonies performed as part of the process of initiation bestow the right to regard property as individual.

I have said enough to show how important a rôle such organizations as these must play in the society of which they form part. They form a highly complicated system, in which political, economic and religious functions are intimately combined. In addition, they form, in many cases, groupings of an educational kind. The process of initiation is not only, in many cases, a period of education in the general knowledge of the community, but the acquirements of special arts, such as the playing of certain instruments and the manufacture of implements or weapons, may form part of the education. Again, ordeals of courage and endurance usually form an essential part of the ritual of initiation, and the tests may be regarded as further examples of the educational function of these organizations. Only one kind of social function is lacking. The organizations have nothing to do with the regulation of marriage, which belongs to the dual or clan organization, which, as a rule, the associations accompany.

The foregoing account has been based mainly on the nature of the organizations of Melanesia. I may now consider how far these features are shared by the voluntary associations of other parts of the world.

Similar organizations are characteristic of West Africa and occur also, though usually in less definite form, in other parts of that continent. One society of West Africa, the Mama Dhiombo, has given its name to our language in the corrupt form of Mumbo Jumbo.

There is hardly a feature of the associations of Melanesia

which is not reproduced in one or other of the societies of Africa. In Africa, as in Melanesia, the proceedings of most of the associations are secret, and are entered by a process of initiation, of which the representation of death and rebirth is an occasional feature. The societies are often linked with the institution of the men's house or the bachelors' house, and in some cases there is definite grading, members rising progressively to higher rank by definite rites. The wearing of masks is frequent, and in some cases they take the form of hats. In only a few cases have the societies been shown to embody a cult of ancestral ghosts, but this is clearly present in some instances ; and the fact that among both the Edo and the Ibo the members who are wearing masks are known as the dead forms an exact parallel with the *tamate* of the Banks Islands.[1]

The making of mysterious sounds to keep uninitiated persons away occurs in Africa, and the bull-roarer is the instrument most frequently used for this purpose. As in Melanesia, many of the societies are connected in some way with animals.

Ordeals and trials of various kinds are regular features of initiation in Africa, and another striking point of similarity with Melanesia is that, both in the Poro societies of the Mendi and Timne, and in the Egbo society of Calabar, property is protected by means of an emblem or symbolic object.

As in Melanesia, membership of most of the societies is confined to men, but there are also women's societies ; and mixed societies composed of both men and women seem to be more definite than in Melanesia.

The only Melanesian feature of which I have found no record in African societies is the obligation to eat only with members of one's own society or of one's own grade in a society.

While nearly all the features of the Melanesian societies are thus found in Africa, there are certain African features which do not occur, or are exceptional, in Melanesia. Thus among the Ibo, there is in some cases a connexion with

[1] Cf. Rivers, *History of Melanesian Society*, s.v. *tamate*.

occupation, the societies thus resembling guilds. It is note-worthy, in relation to the position of smiths elsewhere in Africa, that the highest grade among the Ibo is named after the blacksmiths.

Another African feature is that the societies are sometimes connected with circumcision, this mutilation forming one of the ordeals to which candidates are submitted.

In Melanesia circumcision, or more properly incision, may co-exist with the fraternities, but in the New Hebrides the rites are distinct. In Rook Island, off the east coast of New Guinea, however, there is a definite association of circumcision with the men's house.

In connexion with these many points of similarity between the fraternities of Melanesia and Africa, I should like to call attention to the fact that, owing to the element of secrecy, it is peculiarly difficult to obtain full records, and we can be confident that if we had a more complete account we should find still closer resemblances between the two regions. As an example of what we may expect, I may mention that, if it had not been for my own visits to Melanesia, and if we had had to rely on the work of Codrington for our knowledge of this region, some of the most striking points of resemblance with Africa would not have appeared. We should not have known, for instance, of the ritual representation of death and rebirth, nor of the protection of property by the emblems of the societies. It is, therefore, far from improbable that further investigation in Africa will reveal the presence there of the one Melanesian feature which appears to be absent in the African societies, viz., the obligation of a member to eat only with those of his own group, and the importance of fire in this connexion.

At the same time it must be noted that it is not unlikely that, under the general heading of fraternities and secret societies, institutions of several kinds have been included, and that further knowledge will enable us to classify these groups. Thus, several of the organizations of Africa, which resemble other secret societies, have to do with magic, and may possibly have as a motive the natural desire for secrecy in connexion with magical proceedings. I obtained a good example of such a group in the Banks Islands in Melanesia, where there are associations, quite distinct from the ghost societies, for the practice of magic and for mutual protection against the magic of others. A man who joins one of these associations not only learns certain magical proceedings, but he also learns how to protect himself against the magic of all other members of the association.

It is probable that these associations have come into existence in imitation of the ghost societies, and, if so, it is not improbable that the magical associations of Africa have had a similar origin.

Another part of the world where secret or esoteric associations are frequent is North America, but there the societies are of many different kinds, and it is only exceptionally that there is any great degree of resemblance with the societies of Melanesia or Africa. Perhaps the closest resemblance is in the case of the Midewiwin society of the central Algonquian tribe of the Ojibway, where, in the rites of initiation, there is a ceremonial representation of death and rebirth. A sea-shell is supposed to be shot into the body of the candidate, who falls to the ground unconscious, and only recovers after he has gone through a representation of coughing up the shell which is supposed to have entered his body.[1]

There is very great variety in the nature and purpose of American societies. Some are military in character; others, at any rate at present, whatever they may once have been, are purely convivial. Many are connected with health, and possess certain therapeutic knowledge which is only obtained by initiation, the Midewiwin, which I have mentioned as having ritual of rebirth, being a society of this kind.

Among the Omaha all persons who have seen a buffalo in a dream become members of the buffalo society, while, in the

[1] W. J. Hoffman, " The Midewiwin or 'Grand Medicine Society' of the Ojibway ": *7th Ann. Rep. Bureau Am. Eth.*, 1891.

north-west, membership of a society is also determined by some kind of mysterious encounter with the animal which gives its name to the society.

The resemblance of the Greek mysteries to the African and Melanesian varieties was probably closer,[1] and there is also an interesting suggestion of resemblance in the presence of the animal masks in some of the cave drawings of palæolithic times.

In addition to the organizations of the kind I have described, secret societies exist elsewhere, often apparently of a quite different character. Thus, there are secret organizations in China, many of which are known to be of recent origin, which have political objects of a revolutionary kind, while others are organizations designed for the secret prosecution of heretical religious practices, the two kinds of society often, as one might expect, passing into one another. We have no evidence that any of them resemble the societies of Melanesia or Africa either in ritual or beliefs.

The well-known secret societies of Italy would also appear to have, at any rate in many cases, some antisocial or criminal purpose, and are organizations to make such purposes more effective.

As regards our own secret societies, I will only point out the connexion of the chief of them, that of the Freemasons, with a definite occupation.

An interesting development in modern America is the occurrence of secret fraternities in the universities, with, outwardly at least, points of resemblance with other secret societies, in that they are entered by a process of initiation and have a ritual.

Leaving the occurrence of these organizations of civilized communities on one side we have a very remarkable distribution of the organizations with which I have been dealing in this chapter, in that they are confined to Melanesia, New Guinea,

---

[1] [Cf. Perry, *Origin of Magic and Religion*, chap. vi.]

the eastern end of Indonesia and Africa, they being especially prominent in West Africa. In America the secret society which most closely resembles those of Africa and Melanesia is that of the Midewiwin, the military and open character of so many of the other American organizations suggesting that they may belong to a different category.

If we base our reasoning on this distribution, we are met by the striking fact that secret organizations having features of ritual which bear a close resemblance to one another are found in three widely separated regions, one consisting of Melanesia, New Guinea, and Eastern Indonesia; a second in Africa and especially in West Africa ; and a third in one region of North America. We have here a very interesting case of a problem which is now especially engaging the attention of ethnologists, namely, whether such close resemblances as are found in these three widely separated regions have come into existence independently, or whether they belong to one culture which at some time or other was widely diffused over the earth, and has only persisted in these three regions. I have no intention of attempting any full consideration of this problem, but I should like to point out one or two facts which may help towards its solution. In Africa there is no question that there has been an invasion of pastoral peoples, who have come into the continent from the east, that is, from Asia, and have greatly modified the culture of Eastern, Southern and Central Africa, producing, among many other results, the widespread military peoples who speak the Bantu family of languages. If these pastoral peoples obliterated the secret organizations which existed on their arrival, we should have an explanation of the absence, or relative infrequency, or organizations of the widespread type in Eastern as compared with West Africa.[1]

Again, we know that there has been a relatively late movement, one which took place in the early centuries of the

---

[1] [This is, of course, only one of the possibilities.]

Christian era, from India into the Malay Archipelago, the influence of which is especially pronounced in the more western islands such as Java, and becomes less obvious as one goes eastwards. If this movement had an action upon the secret organizations similar to that of the pastoral invaders of Africa, we have an explanation of the absence of these organizations over a large part of the regions intervening between Melanesia and West Africa.

The American case is more difficult. There are two possibilities ; one that the societies have undergone a special development in North America, so that the Midewiwin alone represents the original institution ; while another possibility is that the peoples who carried the cult over the world only found their way to the Plains, and failed to influence other parts of the continent, a problem the solution of which would take us too far to be considered here.[1]

I will finish this chapter with a brief consideration of the theories of origin of these organizations. One is that they arose as the means of practising religious rites which had been forbidden by rulers, a motive which seems to have been definitely present in the case of many of the secret societies of China, while it has also been supposed to have been the motive of the witches' organizations which are said to have been widespread in Europe.[2] In each case the societies embody an early religious cult which has been thrust into the background by rulers, who had either brought a new religion into there from elsewhere, or had adopted a new religion. According to this view the witches' cult of our own in other European countries is the survival of a pre-Christian religion.

A different view, for which I am responsible, was put forward especially to explain the nature of the organizations of Melanesia. It is that Melanesian secret societies embody the religious cults of immigrants who, coming in small numbers

[1] See Appendix III.
[2] M. A. Murray, *The Witch Cult in Western Europe*, Oxford, 1921.

among an alien people, practised their religion in secret, and only gradually admitted the indigenous people to participation in their rites.[1]

I was led to this view, so far as Melanesia is concerned, by finding that the features which are prominent in the organization and rites of the Melanesian fraternities form, in other islands of Melanesia, part of the social organization and of the open religious cult. I have supposed that, while, in some parts of Melanesia, the religious and political ideals of the immigrants came to be practised in secret, they had elsewhere a more general influence, and were embodied in the general culture of the people among whom the immigrants settled. Thus, the cult of ancestral ghosts, which is the essential religious element in the societies of the New Hebrides and the Banks Islands forms, in the Solomon Islands, the equally essential basis of the religious cult which is practised by all. Again, the definite hereditary chieftainship of the Solomons has, according to this point of view, found expression in the hierarchy formed by the graded associations of the New Hebrides and Banks Islands. It is the persons who stand at the head of this hierarchy who are the only representatives of anything which can be called chieftainship in these islands.

Again, the sanction given to private ownership, which rests in the Solomons upon the cult of ancestral ghosts, forms part, in Southern Melanesia, of the social functions of the ghost societies and graded organizations.

This kind of scheme, devised to explain the special conditions of the Melanesian associations, will also serve to explain those of Africa, if we assume people with a culture similar to that possessed by the immigrants who initiated the associations of Melanesia also found their way to Africa. This supposition will not only explain the many points of close resemblance between the organizations of the two regions, but it will also serve to explain their differences. If the associations of

---

[1] See *The History of Melanesian Society*, chap. xxiv, for a detailed discussion of this matter.

Melanesia and Africa are the outcome of the influence of two parts of a widespread cultural diffusion, it is not to be expected that this common influence would have exactly the same result in places differing so much from one another as the continent of Africa and the islands of Melanesia. If the associations of Africa and Melanesia have arisen out of the common element provided by the beliefs and sentiments of the same movement, the surprising feature is that differences of environment and lapse of time should have allowed so close a resemblance between the two institutions.

I should like now to say a word about an alternative view of the nature of secret societies, which has received wide currency through the book of Professor Hutton Webster.[1] According to this writer, secret societies have arisen through a special development of totemic clans. I believe that there is a grain of truth in this view, but that the way in which it has been expressed by Hutton Webster is open to grave objection. That there is a relation between totemism and the organizations which I have been describing seems to be fairly certain, but, according to my point of view, it is false to suppose that a definite form of social grouping such as a secret society has grown out of another highly organized form of social grouping such as a totemic clan-organization. I suppose rather that fraternities and totemic clans are two different manifestations of beliefs and sentiments carried over the world by people possessing a similar culture. Just as I suppose that the people who, in one place, became chiefs, were, in other places, the founders of secret organizations whose leaders took the place of chiefs, so do I suppose that the men whose beliefs and sentiments produced the ritual of the fraternities in some places became elsewhere the ancestors of totemic clans. It is a striking fact that, wherever secret societies exist in Melanesia, totemism is absent, or of a very indefinite kind ; and it was this fact of distribution which first

[1] *Primitive Secret Societies.*

led me to the view that the two institutions are only different manifestations of one and the same influence.

AGE-GRADES

It will now be convenient to consider a social group of a different, though related kind, one known as an " age-grade ".

In some parts of the world there are social groups, the composition of which depends either upon the period during which the members are born, or upon the time at which they undergo certain rites, especially that of circumcision. These groups are usually known as age-grades, though this term should perhaps be limited strictly to the grouping of the first kind. A good instance of this variety occurs on the east coast of New Guinea, the chief example having been recorded at Bartle Bay. At this place the male children born in every period of about two years form a group which is called a *kimta*.[1] There is no ceremony of admission to a *kimta*, membership being determined altogether by the time of birth. The whole community will thus be divided into a large number of groups differing in age. Thus, in a community where the oldest man is seventy years of age, there may be as many as thirty-five *kimta*.

It would appear from Seligman's account that there are similar *kimta* groups composed of women. The *kimta* have nothing to do with the regulation of marriage, but their members have the obligation of mutual helpfulness, assisting one another in hunting, building, and other occupations, and they eat together at feasts.

A *kimta* extends over a wide area, but members of a *kimta* who live in the same settlement are still more closely linked together as *eriam*.[2] To a great extent *eriam* have their property in common, and each member of an *eriam* group has rights of access to the wives of any of his fellows, communism in property being thus accompanied by sexual communism of a definite

[1] C. G. Seligman, *The Melanesians of British New Guinea*, pp. 470-7, 614-16.
[2] Op. cit., pp. 468-70, 472-7.

kind. Moreover, the *eriam* relation involves the use of classificatory terms of relationship, a child classing with his father all the *eriam* of his father. There is thus a striking similarity with the relationship which exists, or has existed, in Melanesia, between the members of the moiety or clan. Relationships which, in Melanesia, are connected with one kind of grouping, are, in this part of New Guinea, separated from one another, and fall to the lot of two different kinds of group, for the *kimta* exist side by side with an organization in clans grouped together to form a dual organization.

Other examples of age-grades are found in Africa, where they exist among the Masai and other Hamitic or half-Hamitic peoples. Here, however, the event which determines membership is not birth but the time of occurrence of circumcision. Thus, all boys who are circumcised at the same time among the Nandi belong to the same *ipinda*, or age-grade.[1] The interval between successive performances of the rite of circumcision is about seven and a half years, and there are seven *ipinda* groups in existence. Within each *ipinda* there are three subdivisions, also grouped according to age, these groups taking their name from the fire or fire-place, each group having the common use of a fire.[2]

A similar grouping occurs among the Masai, where membership is also dependent on the time of circumcision. Those circumcised during a period of about four years make up one age, and two such ages make a generation. As among the Nandi, each age has three divisions.[2]

In Africa, as in New Guinea, the members of the same age should help one another, and, in the case of the Nandi, this duty seems to be especially incumbent upon members of the same fire. There is also evidence that members of the same fire have right of access to one another's wives.[3]

---

[1] A. C. Hollis, *The Nandi*, Oxford, 1905, pp. 11 sqq.
[2] Id., *The Masai*, p. 261.
[3] Id., *The Nandi*, p. 12.

Among another people, the Suk, Mr. Barton has found an association between the grades and animals resembling in many respects that characteristic of totemism.

Social groups graded according to age also occur in North America, as among the Hidatsa, and this case is one of especial interest, because Lowie has been able to trace out their mode of origin. The age-grades of the Hidatsa resemble in many respects the military fraternities of adjacent regions, but with the difference that, whereas elsewhere men are initiated into these fraternities individually, among the Hidatsa they enter in groups of, or about, the same age, and those admitted at one time form the group which resembles the age-grade of other parts of the world. Lowie supposes that at one time men entered the fraternities of the Hidatsa individually by purchase, and were assisted in obtaining the necessary contributions by their friends. This evolved into a process whereby many men helped one another, and formed a group who were initiated at the same time. Looked at from this point of view, the age-grade is only a special development of the fraternity.

The close relation between the age-grades of North America and the fraternities of that continent naturally leads one to inquire whether a similar relation exists in Africa and New Guinea. In this connexion one striking feature of the age-grades of the Nandi may be mentioned. In comparing the fraternities of Africa with those of Melanesia, we found that only one Melanesian feature is absent in Africa, namely the use of a common fire. This feature which was absent so long as we confined our attention to African fraternities now turns up as part of the equipment of an African age-grade.

The definite association of the age-grades of Africa with circumcision forms another point of resemblance with the fraternities of that continent, and still another point of contact is the connexion of the age-grades of the Suk with animals, both fraternities and age-grades being thus brought into a certain similarity to totemism, in that animals are connected with a form of social grouping. These points of resemblance suggest a definite relation of some kind between fraternities and age-grades in Africa similar to that which had been shown by Lowie to exist in North America.

The age-grade of New Guinea, on the other hand, seems to be of a different order. In the first place it differs from the African institution in depending on the act of birth, and not on a process of initiation. In other words, while the African age-grade is of the voluntary kind, at any rate in so far as the time at which circumcision is performed is voluntary, the age-grade of New Guinea is a very definite example of a grouping of the involuntary kind. The question therefore arises whether there is anything in common to the so-called "age-grades" of Africa and New Guinea. It may be noted also that, while both fraternities and African age-grades are not known to be groupings of the domestic order, this feature is a characteristic of the Papuan institution. The age grouping sets up relationship of the same kind as those determined by the dual or clan grouping.

While the age-grades of Africa and New Guinea seem thus to be wholly unrelated to one another, the study of African age-grades has only served to enhance and add to the many points of resemblance between the voluntary groupings of Africa and Melanesia. These resemblances are so numerous and so close as to leave little doubt that, in spite of the great distance which separates these two parts of the world, the features of their fraternities must have been determined by some common influence.

CHAPTER VIII

OCCUPATION, CLASS, AND CASTE

CHAPTER VIII

Occupation, Class, and Caste

I PROPOSE now to deal chiefly with occupational forms of social grouping, thus leading to one of the economic aspects of society. This subject will bring into prominence two important modes of social grouping about which it is desirable to have a somewhat clearer view than is usually provided by works on sociology. I refer to class and caste. These two terms are often used loosely as interchangeable with one another, Lowie, for instance, being an offender in this respect, and this loose usage is frequent in popular language, for we speak of a person losing caste when we mean that he falls in that social estimation which forms so large an element in the maintenance of class distinctions.

I propose to confine the term " caste " to the well-known institution of India, and to such other examples as it is possible to put into the same category. I shall deal with caste more fully after I have treated occupation, and shall begin by trying to make clear the sense in which we may profitably use the term " class ". I will begin by considering a form of social grouping which may be regarded as a typical example of class. Wherever we find the institution of hereditary chieftainship or kingship, we find also that all the relatives of the chief or king have a privileged position. They are distinguished from other members of the society by special honorific names or prefixes, and have customs peculiar to themselves. The most convenient term for such a group is " noble ", and this term may also be used for those who have a similar privileged position, even though they are not related to the chief or king.

Such a group forms the most characteristic example of a class.

The degree in which the group is marked off from the rest of the community differs in various societies. Thus, to take two examples from Europe, the group of nobles in Germany distinguished by the prefix " von " forms, or formed before the war, a strictly delimited patrilineal group, the sons of a man of this class always belonging to the class, while it was only exceptionally that ordinary members of society were elevated into the noble class. Among ourselves, on the other hand, there is no such strict delimitation, descendants of the noble class continually merging into the general body of the community, while promotions into this class are more frequent than in Germany.

Sometimes the group of nobles is more or less strictly endogamous, the son of a noble having to marry the daughter of another, and only the children of such unions belong to the noble class, In other cases, where mixed marriages are allowed, membership of the class may be determined in the male or female line, the son of a noble man and a women of the commoners being noble in the one case, while in the second case the son of a commoner by a noble wife belongs to the class of his mother.

Often the class of nobles is graded, forming ranks within the class. Our own nobility forms a good example of one kind of grading, while in Polynesia grading depends on purity of noble blood, children both of whose parents are noble ranking above those only one of whose parents is noble. In the Hawaiian Islands the highest kind of noble is one who is the offspring of a union between own brother and sister of the noble class, whose parents were again own brother and sister.

A second example of a class, which is found in many parts of the world, is that of the landowners. Among ourselves landowners merge into the noble class at one end of the scale, and into the ordinary population at the other, but in societies such as those of Fiji and Polynesia, the landowners form a definite class distinguished from the chiefs and nobles.

The office of chief passes insensibly, on the one hand, into that of priest and, on the other, into that of the warrior ; and priests and warriors form characteristic examples of the transition to occupations, the practitioners of which may be regarded as classes, since they often occupy a privileged position similar to that of the nobles. Where the functions of chiefs are purely religious, there may be no distinction between the classes of noble and priest ; and where nobles are especially concerned with the art of war, which seems largely to have been the case in many parts of Polynesia,[1] there is no distinction between the noble class and the class or occupation of warrior. Elsewhere, as among the Masai of Africa, the warriors form a group distinguished from the old men, on the one hand, and from the young men, on the other, thus furnishing a group where class merges into the special form of social grouping known as the age-grade (see p. 137).

In the case of the priesthood we have a definite form of social grouping, in which certain members of the community form a group marked off from the rest by social functions connected with religion. Several varieties of the priesthood can be distinguished. One form is so frequent, and has in many societies become so important, that it is now customary to classify its members apart from priests as *Shamans*. Persons so classified are distinguished by the important part played in their functions, by the belief in possession by spirits, and by the utilization of the belief in practice. The shaman leads us naturally towards two other forms of social group, those composed of magicians, on the one hand, and leeches, on the other. I do not propose to enter here upon the vexed subject of the distinction between religion and magic, between the priest, whose social functions are to bring men into relation

---

[1] [This is only true of later times. See Perry, *The Children of the Sun*, chap. xi.]

with the gods or other higher powers, on the one hand, and the sorcerer whose social, or perhaps more correctly, anti-social, function it is to bring disease and death upon members of the community.[1]   In many cases there is a sharp distinction between the two, but intermediate gradations are numerous ; and at present we know too little about the exact nature of the social functions of the two groups to enable us to define their status.   Similar transitions are found between medicine and religion, but in this case the clearly marked business of the one to deal with disease enables us to consider this kind of grouping more closely.   In speaking of this form of social grouping, it is convenient to use the terms " leech " and " leechcraft " for the person and institution whose social function it is to deal with disease.   In some cases the leech is also a priest, the attitude towards disease being closely bound up with that towards the gods or other higher powers, and a close relation, if not identity, of social function between the two professions occurs in Indonesia, Polynesia, and North America.   In other cases, the social functions of the leech are closely related to those of the sorcerer ; while in other cases again, his functions are connected with those of the barber, as in Morocco and other parts of Northern Africa, an association of which the barber-surgeons of our own history form a characteristic example, the association probably going back to a time when both bleeding and shaving were processes which were quite as much religious or magical as medical or æsthetic.   In a few simple societies, as in those of Indonesia, there has come about the definite differentiation of the leech from other occupations which is characteristic of our own civilization.[2]

One feature of the social groups connected with religion, magic and medicine, which should be mentioned here, is that they are often entered by a definite process of initiation, in

---

[1] Sorcery can have its good side as well.   See *The History of Melanesian Society*, chap. xxxiii.

[2] Perry, *The Megalithic Culture of Indonesia*, chap. xviii.

which the candidate is exposed to ordeals, or has to go through periods of fasting, seclusion, or other trials, while in some cases the process of initiation has characters which show that it is symbolic of death and rebirth. I must be content here only to remind the reader that this feature is generally present in fraternities or secret societies (see Chap. VII).

The consideration of the transitions from definite classes, through the priesthood, to other groups with social functions of a different kind, leads to the strictly economic aspect of occupation. The examples I have given have led, by natural transitions, to so definite an occupation as that of the barber. In other words, classes pass by insensible gradations into crafts and other forms of occupation. In our own society there is sometimes a definite relation between occupation and class, the followers of some occupations having special privileges and taking a higher place in social estimation than others.

I have so far been considering occupational groupings in their relation to class. It is now time to turn to other aspects of these groupings. I will begin with a reference to occupation in connexion with sex. The general rule throughout the world is that certain occupations are regarded as proper to men, others as proper to women, while others, again, may be followed by both sexes. The occupations which I have already considered are by no means limited to men, women being in many places prominent as priests, shamans, or leeches. A good example of the definite sharing of occupations in a simple community comes from the Polynesian island of Tikopia, where house-building, most kinds of fishing, and certain specialized occupations, to be considered shortly, are followed by men, while women cook and make bark-cloth and mats.[1]

Looking after cattle throughout the world is usually the work of men, while, in agriculture, the usual rule is that the bulk of the work is done by women, the men only intervening to carry out the more difficult or arduous tasks, such as cutting down trees and clearing the ground, which bulk largely in the

[1] *The History of Melanesian Society*, i, p. 325.

agriculture of those peoples who only use a plot of ground for a limited time and then allow it to relapse into wildness.

Certain specializations of industry according to sex are widely found throughout the world. Thus, canoe building is almost always, if not invariably, confined to men, while the art of making pottery by hand is almost universally practised by women, men only following this occupation when the potter's wheel is used. A rule of wide application is that occupations involving religious ritual, i.e. involving knowledge of manual or verbal rites implying appeal to higher powers, are practised by men, while occupations devoid of this sacred aspect are open to women.

Great variations occur in the degree of specialization of occupation among different members or groups of a society. Sometimes division of labour seems to be absent, all arts and crafts being followed by every member of the population, except for the differences according to sex already mentioned. It is a striking fact that, when division of social function first appears, it is often in connexion with religion or the closely allied leechcraft. Thus, in Eddystone Island in the Solomons, where most arts are practised by all, there is a high degree of specialization of function in relation to disease and its treatment. In that island it is believed that each recognized disease arises through the infraction of a taboo, which I have mentioned (see p. 113), as a means of assigning the fruit of certain trees to individual use. There are nearly a hundred such taboos, each with its special ritual and confined to a small group of practitioners, sometimes to one only. Since the disease dependent upon infraction of each taboo can only be cured by a man who knows the appropriate rites, there has arisen a state of affairs in which each disease has its own specialists, leading to a degree of specialism in leechcraft exceeding that of modern medicine. In other cases, where occupation is specialized, it would seem that this has arisen out of religious rather than practical needs. Thus, in Ambrim in the New Hebrides, certain men called *meteso* have the specialized function of making canoes, gongs and other objects which involve carving, while other occupations such as fishing, agriculture and house-building are practised by all, the only differentiation in these occupations being in the special parts of a craft assigned to men and women respectively. The process of making canoes and gongs is far more than a merely practical art, and is accompanied throughout by ritual of a religious kind, apparently designed to appease spirits and ancestral ghosts, including the spirit of the tree, or some ancestral ghost believed to be resident in the tree, from which the canoe is made. It therefore constitutes an instance of the differentiation of occupation according to sex.

In the little Polynesian island of Tikopia, and throughout Polynesia generally, the canoe-makers form a special group of craftsmen.[1] The ceremonial character of the process of manufacture, and the importance attached to the formulæ uttered at its different stages, suggest that the special position of the craftsmen is due to their religious knowledge and prestige rather than to their material skill. In Tikopia there are only two other specialized crafts, tattooing and the manufacture of tumeric,[2] while in other parts of Polynesia the number of crafts may be much larger, there being nine specialized occupations in Tonga, viz. the canoe-makers, the cutters of whale-tooth ornaments, superintendents of funeral rites, stone-masons, net-makers, fishermen, house-builders, tattooers, carvers of clubs, barbers, cooks, and peasants.[3] Throughout Polynesia the people who follow specialized occupations are called *tufunga*, and it is noteworthy that this word also denotes a priest, pointing clearly to the importance attached to the religious aspects of the arts and crafts.

In general these specialized crafts are hereditary, but, in some cases, there may be some kind of apprenticeship, or

[1] *The History of Melanesian Society*, i, p. 326.
[2] Id., pp. 327, 328.
[3] W. Mariner, *An Account of the Natives of the Tonga Islands*, 1817, ii, pp. 93, 96, 274.

admittance to a craft may depend on some kind of test or
ordeal.   Thus, in the island of Tikopia, a man who wishes to
become a canoe-maker will make a model in the bush, and, if
he is successful, he may gradually become a professional
craftsman or *tufunga*.   The fact that, in some parts of Oceania,
the art of canoe-making has disappeared, suggests that the
craft is often purely hereditary, so that it would disappear
if the family-group which practised it happened to die out.

Sometimes certain occupations are hereditary and others
not.   Thus, in Tonga, all the crafts I have enumerated were
hereditary, except those of tattooing and club-making, which
might or might not be so.

Sometimes certain crafts could only be followed by persons
of a certain rank.   Thus, in Tonga, where there were classes
intermediate between the nobles and the lowest grade of
commoner, certain occupations, such as canoe-making, were
limited to those of the higher ranks, while shaving and cooking
were only practised by persons from the lowest class.[1]   This
distinction would seem to be connected with the sacred
character of certain occupations.

It is noteworthy that the canoe-makers stand at the head
of the occupations of Tonga, and this position is almost
certainly due to the sacred character of the craft, and to the
importance of the rites, manual and verbal, which accompany
the manufacture.

Similar groupings of persons following definite crafts occur
in America, this feature being especially developed in the
ancient civilizations of Mexico and Central America.   These
groupings were not confined to men, developed associations
for the practice of various occupations having been observed,
in the United States, among the women of the Cheyenne,
entrance to the membership of each association being attained
only by the payment of heavy entrance fees.   These
occupational associations have many points of resemblance

---

[1] Mariner, op. cit.

with the guilds of our mediæval history, and with the trade unions of the present day. Where the occupations are hereditary, these associations will often necessarily coincide with some form of the various family groupings already considered, usually, it would seem, with some form of the joint-family. When the associations are not hereditary, but are entered by means of special payments, or by a process of apprenticeship, they will form groupings of the voluntary kind, and will cut across domestic groupings like the family and clan. In such cases they form important factors in producing an increase of social complexity. In most parts of the world occupational groupings, even if hereditary, are not associated with strict endogamy, men who follow a craft being allowed to take their wives from groups following crafts of a different kind. There is, however, a frequent tendency to endogamy in connexion with occupation, for marriages to occur between the children of parents who follow the same craft, partly due to the close associations which follow from common occupation, partly from a desire not to endanger craft secrets by unions with women from uninitiated groups. The tendency towards such endogamous unions is clearly to be observed among ourselves, especially in connexion with such crafts as that of the fisherman. In general, however, the endogamy is not organized, though there is evidence that it once existed in a definite form in some of the guilds from which our city companies are derived. With these exceptions, endogamy is not a necessary feature of the social groups formed by persons following a common craft, except in two parts of the world, Africa and India. In Africa, the association of endogamy with craft-groups occurs especially in connexion with the occupation of smiths or workers in metal. Among the Masai, Gallas, and other Hamitic, or partially Hamitic, peoples, the smiths form a distinct group, whose marriages are confined strictly within their own body. In many cases, especially among the Masai, the smiths have physical and linguistic characters which suggest that they were once, or are even still, a distinct people, the Andarobo.[1] It is probable that these endogamous craft-groups are indigenous peoples who, when a warrior class settled in their country, were given a definite status owing to the usefulness of their occupation, but were not admitted to such intimacy as would be associated with intermarriage. They thus came to form a group kept apart from the rest of the community by means of endogamy.

CASTE

In India, on the other hand, the practice of endogamy is not only strictly organized, but, wherever the caste-system has been adopted, it applies, with certain exceptions, to the whole community. Here, as in Africa, the endogamy is associated with occupation, but the Indian differs from the African institution in its highly organized and obligatory character, as well as in its application to all branches of the community which practise it. Two of the special features of the caste-system of India thus are its highly organized character, and the association of endogamy with occupation. Another feature is that the castes, thus segregated from one another by endogamy and occupation, are arranged in a hierarchical series, with the more or less sacred caste of the Brahmins at their head. Still another feature is that this hierarchical arrangement is associated with rules of avoidance of various kinds, and also with regulations of other kinds concerning the relations to one another of the different castes. These rules are especially definite in relation to food. In many cases a person may only take food, at any rate food of certain kinds, which has been prepared by members of his own caste, these rules applying with different degrees of strictness according to the nature of the food, and especially according to the way in which it has been cooked. This not only holds good in the higher castes, but may be followed quite as rigorously by castes which take a relatively low place in the hierarchy.

[1] Hollis, *The Masai*, p. 330, n. 1.

Another group of rules of avoidance apply to personal contact. These rules have been especially developed in Malabar, where the order of precedence receives a quantitative character in terms of the distance which members of various castes must keep from a Brahmin. Thus, a Nayar may not approach within six paces of a Nambutiri Brahmin ; a man of the barber caste not within twelve paces ; a carpenter or goldsmith not within twenty-four. For a Tiyyan the distance is thirty-six ; for a Mayayan sixty-four ; and for a Polayan ninety-six paces.

These rules concerning personal contact have been classed by the French writer, Bouglé,[1] with the rule of endogamy, as examples of the mutual repulsion of castes, but there is the striking difference between the two that, whereas infringement of the rules concerning food and contact are not irremediable, and persons put out of their caste for their infraction may be readmitted, the marriage regulation is treated far more strictly, and persons who have married out of their castes find themselves permanently excluded.

The four main features of the caste-system are, therefore, endogamy, hereditary occupation, hierarchical character, and rules of avoidance between different members of the hierarchy, especially in relation to food and contact. Some of these features, however, are more theoretical than real, and this is especially the case in relation to occupation. If the rule of hereditary occupation had been strictly followed, we should find that all Brahmins are priests, and all Kshattriyas rulers or warriors, but, as a matter of fact, this is very far from being the case. There are hardly any occupations which are not now followed by a Brahmin except those which are directly contaminating, such as leather-dressing or spirit-selling, and a similar variety of occupation occurs in many other castes. In fact, the variety of occupation has become so great that it has been possible for an Indian scholar, Guru

[1] C. Bouglé, "Remarques sur le régime des castes": *L'année Sociologique,* iv, 1901.

Proshad Sen, to sum up the features of caste and leave out occupation altogether, while, according to other Indian scholars, the rôle of occupation in the history of caste has been greatly exaggerated. It is probable, however, that, at one time, not perhaps at first, hereditary occupation was one of the leading features of caste ; and even now it is far from easy for a man to give up the occupation of his own caste and take to another, except one of those which have come into existence as the result of British influence.

Another noteworthy feature of the caste-system is that most of the larger bodies, such as the Brahmins, which are usually regarded as castes, are really groups of castes, and these groups may be very numerous. Thus the Brahmins now form a vast number of castes distinguished from one another, partly by difference of locality, partly by difference of occupation. The rule of endogamy applies to groups very small in size as compared with the general body of Brahmins. This is probably due in large measure to movements from one part of India to another. A body of Brahmins who moved from one place to another became a new endogamous group, and, in effect, a new caste.

I have as yet said nothing about certain Indian practices which, being intimately associated with the caste-system, are usually regarded as among its constituent elements. I refer to such customs as infant marriage and the prohibition of the remarriage of widows. These are not, however, necessary features of caste, and can disappear without affecting the essential character of the system.

One feature of the caste-system which may be mentioned is that it is continually growing by the inclusion within it of tribes which once stood without the system. This process is going on at present, and has probably been in action for a long time. This point is of interest in connexion with the problem of the origin of caste, with a brief consideration of which I will conclude this chapter.

The problem to be solved is this. Why has India become the

seat of so highly specialized an example of the association of endogamy and occupation, and why has the group formed by those especially acquainted with the sacred lore become the head of the hierarchy ?   Most Anglo-Indian writers have laid especial stress upon the segregation of occupation, which occurs in many parts of the world, as the basis of caste, while others, including many Indian scholars, have rather stressed the power of the Brahmin, due to his special knowledge of religious belief and rite, leading to his dominance over the rest of the population.   A third point of view, first put forward by the French writer Sénart, is that the caste-system of India is a special result of the contact of peoples, and has been the outcome of the interaction between invaders having certain religious beliefs, and especially one in the necessity of cere-monial purity in the performance of their religious rites, and an indigenous population, the members of which were only allowed to adopt the introduced cult in a subordinate position, and with certain restrictions on their intercourse with the strangers.   Especially important in this interaction was the belief of the invaders in the essential need for purity of blood as a necessary condition for the proper performance of religious ceremonial, so that the offspring of mixed marriages, i.e. of marriages between immigrant men and indigenous women, were not admitted to equality with the pure-blooded children of the invaders, but came to form groups or castes of lower rank, while the feature, already mentioned, by which indigenous tribes were admitted to still lower ranks in the system, formed another means by which caste grew in magnitude and permeated almost every part of India.   According to this point of view, the four primary castes of Indian history, the Brahmins as priests or singers ;   the Kshattriyas as rulers and warriors ; the Vaisyas as merchants and husbandmen ; and the Sudras as the servile element or labourers of the immigrants, were not primarily castes, but rather classes of the immigrants who came to form the basis of the caste-system through their special mode of interaction with the aboriginal population of India.

If this be so, if the classes of an invading people only became castes as a result of their interaction with the indigenous population of India, it becomes of great importance to make the distinction insisted upon at the beginning of this chapter between class and caste, and not, as is often done, to use the two terms indifferently.

Another special feature of the caste-system of India is that it forms an intimate blend of modes of social grouping which among ourselves are separate, or are, at least, more easily distinguished from one another. As an instrument for the regulation of marriage caste, in the first place, forms a mode of social grouping of the kind I have called domestic, though one in which many functions of the domestic grouping have come to be connected with the subsidiary groupings of the joint family and the joint household. In the second place, through its connexion with occupation, it is a grouping of the economic kind, and has economic functions of great importance. Thirdly, through the predominant position of the Brahmins, and, to a less extent, of the Kshattriyas, or their modern representatives, the Rajputs, caste has political functions of great importance ; while a fourth aspect of caste, perhaps more important than any other, is its function as a religious grouping. One feature of caste of great interest to the student of social institutions, is the predominance of religious influence. One of the outstanding features of the history of human society is the frequent occurrence, at one stage or another, of a struggle between the ecclesiastical and civil powers, between the political and religious forms of social grouping. In advanced civilizations other than that of India, the civil power has in general gained the mastery ; but caste seems to provide a case where this mastery has fallen to the religious side, a grouping primarily religious having acquired functions which elsewhere fall to the lot of groups of a political order. The predominance of a mode of social grouping whose primary functions were religious gives a special interest to the caste-system of India.

CHAPTER IX

GOVERNMENT

CHAPTER IX

GOVERNMENT

BEFORE I enter upon the subject of government, in the sense in which the term is ordinarily understood, it may be instructive to consider briefly the mode of exerting authority in the different forms of domestic grouping. It has already been seen, when considering mother-right, that, in the case of the family in the strict sense, the subject of authority is by no means simple. Authority may be divided between the father and the mother's brother, that of the latter being often the greater; or it may be divided between the mother and her brothers; or, in exceptional cases, it may rest with the mother. Again, in some societies, of which that of France is an example, the authority of the head of the family may be greatly influenced by, or definitely subject to, the decisions of a family council.

For the joint family, I will take as my examples the different forms of this mode of grouping in India. In the patrilineal joint family of Bengal the eldest male member, called *karta*, is the head. His authority is absolute, and is not circumscribed by any kind of council. In the patrilineal joint family of other parts of India, where the *mitakshara* system prevails, brothers usually separate, and set up establishments of their own, and there is no such recognized head of the family as the *karta* of Bengal; but, in practice, the father is an autocrat. It may be mentioned that, though the eldest brother has no legal authority, he has nevertheless great prestige, if not power, with the rest of the joint family, in that he is the possessor of the family gods. Other members of the group have to pay him reverence before performing religious ceremonies, while he only may make the appropriate offerings at a funeral ceremony.

In the matrilineal joint family of Malabar, the senior male member, who is called *karanavan*, is the legal guardian of every member of the *taravad*, over the property of which he has absolute control.[1]

We have little evidence concerning the exertion of authority in the kindred. In the case I know best, that of Eddystone Island in the Solomons, the group has no member in whom any kind of authority is vested, the older members being probably the more influential if any problem arises which needs the exertion of authority.

Authority in the clan is also a subject about which our information is defective. Occasionally the clan may have a headman, but usually there is no one person in the clan who exerts more authority than the rest, except as the result of age or prestige.[2]

It is in connexion with the tribe that the subject of authority becomes of special importance, and takes a form which justifies us in speaking of government. In tribal societies we can discern, at first sight, three main varieties of government : one in which authority is vested in one or two persons, giving us the institution of chieftainship or kingship, single or dual, the powers of which may, or may not, be limited by some kind of council ; a second, in which authority is vested in a council ; and a third, in which authority is in the hands of a few, who may be either a body of hereditary nobility, or may attain their prominent position by age or wealth. When we learn to know these various forms of government in simple societies, we find, in many cases, a state of affairs in which such words as " chief " and " government " mean something very different from that which they ordinarily bear. It will be

---

[1] F. Fawcett, *Bull. Madras Government Museum*, 1901, iii, p. 237.

[2] [The usual rule is that the clan has a council, consisting of the senior members, usually men, which transacts all its business.]

the principal task of this chapter to try to make clear the nature of the institution we call chieftainship in many human societies, and the nature of the process of government in the absence of any definite person in whom authority is vested.

As a characteristic example of the kind of institution which is found in many parts of the world, I may take the chieftainship of Eddystone Island in the Solomons, which I have already mentioned on several occasions. This island is the seat of an institution which, at first sight, seems to correspond closely with our concept of chieftainship, and has, as a matter of fact, been thought so to correspond by the British protectorate of the islands. There are certain persons called *bangara*, occupying a prominent position, which they transmit to their children, who are regarded with respect, if not even with reverence, by the society in general. In other words, the island appears at first sight to provide a characteristic example of hereditary chieftainship. On investigation, however, it was found that these so-called chiefs exerted none of the social functions which we ordinarily associate with chieftainship. It is a question whether these " chiefs " had anything to do with government in the sense in which we understand the term. They held no courts before which offenders were brought, nor had they any special position in connexion with the administration of justice. They had important functions in connexion with war, in that they had the chief voice in deciding when a head-hunting expedition should be organized, but they were not the leaders in the expedition when it set out. Even if a *bangara* accompanied an expedition, he was not expected to be its leader. It was only in connexion with the more ceremonial or religious aspects of warfare that the " chief " was important, and this gives the clue to his special position, for it was in the ordering of ceremonial, and in the arrangement of the feasts which formed important features of this ceremonial, that he was especially prominent.

This aspect of a chief's function was well exemplified by the chief with whom we had most to do in Eddystone. Though his proper name was Rembo, we found that he was habitually called Kikere, or bad, and we were told that he was definitely regarded as a bad chief.   We expected to hear tales of his injustice or cruelty, of his arbitrary ways of government or of the severity of the punishments he inflicted, but in place of these we heard only the complaint that he gave few feasts, and these lacking in quality.   The social function which stood out prominently in the people's minds was the arrangement and provision of feasts.

These features of Eddystone society may be summed up in the statement that its chieftainship was a religious rather than a political institution, and when we pass from Melanesia to Polynesia we find that the sacred character of the chief or king is so pronounced that it seems to be impracticable for him to exert such of his functions as would bring him into contact with the common people, so that another kind of chief, especially associated with war, is associated with him, producing the dual chieftainship characteristic of many parts of Polynesia. In some parts of the Pacific, as in the Hawaiian Islands, this dual feature seems to have been absent, the institution of chieftainship having developed into a form of kingship not greatly different from that of our own society.[1]   In other places, as in the Tongan Islands, the sacred chief or *tuitonga* seems to have had his position and powers obscured by the existence of chiefs of other kinds.[2]

A dual chieftainship similar to that of Polynesia occurs in some parts of New Guinea.   Thus, among the Mekeo people, each clan possesses two chiefs, the high chief and the war chief, while, among the Roro peoples, the high chief was associated with another, whose business it was to see that the orders of the high chief were obeyed.   In these cases the functions of the high chief were mainly of a sacred kind. He could impose taboos, and was able to bring about peace

---

[1] [See, however, Fornander, *An Account of the Polynesian Race*, pp. 41–4.]

[2] Mariner, *An Account of the Natives of the Tonga Islands*, pp. 83–4.

in case of war, but entirely by religious or magico-religious means, such as the scattering of lime or the waving of a bough of a dracaena tree ; while the ordering of feasts formed, as in Eddystone, an important part of his functions. The two kinds of chief among the Roro peoples were called chiefs of the right and left respectively, from the position which they occupied in the common clubhouse during ceremonial.[1]

There is little doubt that in Japan we have an institution of a similar kind. When a king becomes so sacred that none of his subjects may look at him, the exertion of any kind of social function becomes difficult ; and it is probable that the seclusion which for several centuries was the fate of the Mikado of Japan was the direct result of his having acquired a character so sacred that the junctions of government essential to the welfare of such a state as Japan had to be exerted by members of another, and more worldly, family.

In Africa we find chieftainship of several different kinds. In some societies the functions of the chief seem to be almost exclusively religious. He often is a rainmaker, sometimes the sole rainmaker of the community over which he rules. In some cases there is no evidence that he exerts any of the social functions which we associate with government. In other parts of Africa the secular powers of the chief have become very great, and his position as wielder of authority far more pronounced than those connected with religion ; but it is noteworthy that, where the chief administers justice, he is usually assisted by a council ; and, according to one recent writer, this assistance is so constant among the Bantu that individual authority in this respect is unknown. There is also much difference of practice in Africa concerning the enforcement of the chief's decisions, the power of enforcement only occasionally resting with the chief. Occasionally, as among the Zulus and in some parts of West Africa, the power of the chief seems to be almost unlimited ; but it is a question

---

[1] Seligman, *The Melanesians of British New Guinea.*

whether this high degree of authority is not of recent growth, possibly even the result, direct or indirect, of our own influence.

One feature of African chieftainship, mentioned in the last chapter, is his frequent position as the owner, or at least the theoretical owner, of the land. It seems clear that nowhere is he regarded as its absolute owner, but rather as the distributor of rights in land among his people.

In North America, despite many superficial differences, the position of the chief appears not to have been very different from that of Melanesia. In one respect his power seems in general to have been more limited, in that he could usually only announce and arrange feasts with the consent of a council. It is probable, however, that the difference is only formal, and that, though there was no formal council, the Melanesian chief only acted with the agreement of other important members of the society. Only one tribe of North America, that of the Natchez of the Lower Mississippi Valley, had concentrated any great degree of authority in the hands of its chiefs, including the right over life and death ; but even here it is probable that the powers of the ruler were limited by the activity of a council and of subordinate village chiefs.

The published accounts of several American societies suggest the presence of a form of chieftainship which I have not so far mentioned, namely, one in which the chief is elected. Thus, as I have already mentioned (see p. 89), it is said that the chiefs of the Iroquois were elected by women, or by a council of which women were important members ; and in other tribes of North America election is said to have been the process by which chiefs attained their office. I am indebted to Dr. Paul Radin for the information that, in these cases, the power of election was not unlimited, but that the choice was confined to the members of certain families, and that, in many cases, the so-called power of election meant nothing more than the decision whether a chief should be succeeded by his son or by a brother, a process for which parallels can certainly be found in Africa, and probably elsewhere.

The general result of this survey is to show that, in many parts of the world, the institution called chieftainship or kingship is unaccompanied by the exertion of real authority or of political functions such as we associate with government in our own country, at any rate, so far as the administration of justice is concerned. The divine right of kings, and the religious aspect of kingship, which long survived, if they do not still survive, in our own society, form the essence of the chieftainship of such regions as Melanesia and Polynesia, as well as of many parts of Africa and America.[1]

Before I leave the subject of chieftainship, I should like to point out that no other feature of simple society suffers such rapid modification under the external influence of the European, which is now permeating all parts of the world. The European official who visits a new region will at once ask for the chief, by which he means a person with whom he can negotiate, and who will act as an intermediary between the people and himself. Sometimes the real chief steps forward, when he comes to wield powers of which till then he had not dreamed, so that the whole institution of chieftainship, as well as the mode of government, soon suffers great modification. In other cases, in response to the demand of the stranger, the place of the chief is taken by some other man, who is thus vested with an authority wholly foreign to the people. In Melanesia authority may thus fall into the hands of one whose position depends on his having paid a visit to Sydney, and his having acquired some pidgin-English, with the result that the representative of the British Government is one who has little prestige, and conducts his business apart from those whom the people regard with reverence.

In Africa European influence seems to have acted in two ways. In some cases it has, as in Melanesia, produced a form of chieftainship with definite authority which was unknown before; while, in other cases, where chieftainship had already

[1] See Sir J. G. Frazer, *The Magic Art and the Evolution of the Kingship.*

developed towards the attainment of real authority in relation
to justice, there has been the opposite effect, and a once
powerful institution of chieftainship has disappeared, leaving
only a number of petty headmen.

If we accept the position that, in many societies where
chieftainship exists, this institution has little or nothing to
do with government, the problem with which we are faced is
to discover how the business of government is conducted. I
have already mentioned that, in many societies possessing the
institution of chieftainship, the power of the chief is limited,
or he is assisted by some kind of council, and that, at any rate
in some cases, this council exerts such functions of government
as are obvious. In other societies a council may perform
functions in connexion with justice or other branches of government. In these societies anything of the nature of chieftainship
may be absent, or one member of the council may merely be
more important than the rest. All gradations are found
between a council of this kind, formally constituted, and
perhaps consisting of persons representing different groups of
the society, to one of a kind so indefinite that it can hardly
be called a council. As examples of the more definite kind,
I may mention the *panchayat* of the Indian village community,[1]
and the corresponding council or *naim* of the Todas,[2] the
members of which represent certain clans of the society. At
the other end of the scale we have, in those parts of Melanesia
which are devoid of chiefs, and also in Australia, the indefinite
group by means of which some vague kind of authority
is exerted.[3] In both these regions authority is especially
exerted by the old men of the society, giving a form of government which may be called a gerontocracy. We know little
about the exact nature or mode of functioning of the group
of elders, but there is little doubt that it is not a body formally
constituted, or marked off from the rest of the society by any

---

[1] S. C. Roy, *The Oraons of Chota Nagpur*, 1915, pp. 406 et seq.
[2] Rivers, *The Todas*, 550.
[3] Howitt, pp. 301 sqq.

sharply marked line. In Melanesia its membership probably depends in many cases on the power of malignant magic, which the old men are believed to possess, while still more definite is the part taken by graded organizations usually, though not altogether accurately, called secret societies, which form a grouping of the utmost importance in the social organization of some parts of Melanesia. Owing either to their position in these societies, or to the belief in their magical powers, the old men may have almost unlimited authority.

It would seem, however, that both here and in those regions where chieftainship carries with it little authority, at any rate in civil matters, there is an absence of any formal machinery of government which a member of a society highly organized in this respect finds difficult to understand ; while the absence of such organization places great difficulties in the way of its study. I may perhaps best illustrate this subject by reference to my own observations in Melanesia, especially in such a society as that of Eddystone Island, where the functions of the chiefs are religious rather than political. I have already said that, in this island, and the same holds good of Melanesia in general, there is no tribunal for the administration of justice, or for the punishment of offences against other individuals or against the community as a whole, but the administration of justice has a spontaneous character which is wholly foreign to our own point of view. I will illustrate by reference to the crime and punishment of Eddystone. In this island certain offences, especially the theft of fruit from trees protected by taboos, are believed to receive punishment at the hands of the ancestral ghosts, and do not enter into the category of crime. So far as one could tell, the only grave offences formerly recognized were incest and murder, meaning by the latter term killing of a person by a member of his own community. For both incest and murder, and especially for the former, the punishment was death. I was unable to discover that the infliction of this punishment took place as the result of any formal decision by chiefs, elders, council, or meeting of the community in general. To my informants it seemed obvious that one who had committed incest would be killed, and that any kind of machinery for the determination of guilt or for reaching a decision concerning punishment was quite unnecessary. The punishment followed automatically the discovery of the crime, and it seemed that the relatives (or *taviti*) of the offender took the leading part in the infliction of the punishment.

For offences of lesser magnitude the punishment was ostracism, of which I may give an example from my own observation. In Eddystone Island it is the rule that a man may only take a second wife if he is a chief, or has taken ten heads in warfare. During our visit to the island a man who had neither of these qualifications took a second wife, and was consequently ostracized or boycotted by the rest of the island. He took the opportunity to spend his time with us, and occupied himself in making a model canoe, which is now in our museum ; but after about ten days he became tired of his isolation, gave up his second wife and returned to his village, to carry for the rest of his life, so far as we could tell, a social stigma for having tried unsuccessfully to regard himself as superior to the traditions of the community. I could not discover that there had been any formal condemnation in this case. The man had committed an offence against the community, and the community had, intuitively it would seem, decided to have no more social dealings with the offender till the offence was purged.

In certain cases punishment lay in the hands of the injured party. Of this also an example occurred during our visit. Eddystone Island is the seat of very strict monogamy, the society differing from that of more civilized parts of the world in that lapses on the part of the man are regarded as strictly as those on the part of the woman. During our visit a man offended, and as soon as the wife discovered the offence, she put a knife into her husband, inflicting a severe, though not fatal, wound. The procedure was regarded as quite orthodox and natural. The man had offended, and the injured wife had taken the obvious course, and that was the end of the matter.

A fourth mode of Melanesian procedure, which, so far as I know, only takes place in connexion with the so-called secret societies, is the infliction of a fine as a punishment for offences against the society.

We may be enabled the better to understand the spontaneous, or, as it might be called, intuitive mode of inflicting punishment by such knowledge as we possess concerning the deliberations of councils or less formal bodies in such regions as Melanesia. In these councils there are none of the formal means of reaching decisions by voting or other means which are customary among ourselves. At a certain stage of the discussion it seems to be recognized by some kind of common sense, which I have elsewhere regarded as part of a gregarious instinct, that the group has reached agreement.[1] The conclusion which has been reached is intuitively known to all, and the meeting passes on to the next business. A friend who has had the opportunity of observing the social activity of the Russian peasants tells me that the same complete absence of governorship and apparently unregulated teaching of conclusions is characteristic of their assemblies. There is much reason to believe that this unwitting or intuitive method of regulating social life is, in many societies at any rate, closely connected with the communism which was considered in Chapter VI, that among such a people as the Melanesians there is a group-sentiment which makes unnecessary any definite social machinery for the exertion of authority, in just the same manner as it makes possible the harmonious working of communal ownership, and ensures the peaceful character of a communistic system of sexual relations.

So far as we know, the presence of this powerful group-sentiment is associated in large measure with the clan

[1] *Instinct and the Unconscious*, pp. 94–6.

organization, of which the accompanying system of the classificatory denotation of relationship is so striking an expression. As I have already pointed out, we are not yet in a position to decide whether this clan organization has been a constant feature of the development of human society. It is possible that some societies have passed directly from the stage of the collecting band to some such form of social organization as that of the patriarchal family, so popular in social theory, free from the powerful group-sentiment of the clan system with its accompanying communistic practices. It is possible that the strong individualism of our own society, and of other societies of mediæval and modern civilization, has escaped, at any rate to a great extent, the influences derived from the possession of a clan organization. Such evidence as we possess, however, suggests that this has not been so, and that the problem which confronts the student of the social and political institutions of modern civilization is to discover how the group-sentiment which makes unnecessary any definite machinery of government, as well as the communistic practices which are so prevalent among the people of existing simple societies, have been so transformed that, to many members of our own society, any principle of social conduct other than " each man for himself " is beyond the reach of their understanding. The members of an individualistic society may be as unable to understand the activity of a tribal council as a member of a communistic society may, as we saw in the last chapter, be unable to understand the concept, to us so simple and obvious, of the sale of land.

If we accept, at any rate provisionally, the position that all human societies have passed through a communistic stage, with all its pervading group-sentiment, if not group-instinct, it becomes the task of the student to discover the mechanism of its transformation. We can now be sure that there has never been anything of the nature of a social contract, to which the acceptance of authority can be ascribed. A people dominated by such a group-sentiment as actuates the Melanesian or the Polynesian could never of themselves reach a situation in which the formulation of a social contract within their own community would have been possible. We can be confident that so powerful a sentiment could only be changed by external influence, and that the change from spontaneous group-action in government to the authority of individuals has been one of the results of the contact and blending of peoples, that it is only the influence of the more enterprising members of another culture, endowed with qualities, material and mental, regarded as superior, which could change communistic and democratic societies with their powerful group-sentiment into individualistic and monarchical or aristocratically governed societies. According to this view we should expect that the enterprising strangers who set the change in motion would become the chiefs of the society of which they had become members, and I will conclude by giving some evidence that this has happened. In many societies the chiefs have customs peculiar to themselves, the nature of which cannot be explained either by their superior rank, or by the necessities of the office of those who practise them. On the other hand, there is often a striking similarity between the customs of the chiefs of different societies, often widely separated in space, which suggests that they are all offshoots of a common stock, which, having entered the different societies, have become their rulers. Thus, in Oceania, the chiefs, in many cases, preserve their dead by some kind of process similar to mummification, while the common people inter their dead, or pay them no particular regard. With this difference is associated the belief that the chiefs go after death to one place, often a home in the sky, while the common people pass to an underground world of the dead. With these and other peculiarities of custom, of which the marriage of brother and sister is a good example, most readily explicable as the practices of an intruding people, one finds in some places differences in physical appearance between chief and commoner, the former approaching more nearly the Caucasian type, and these differences are often accompanied by traditions of an explicit kind that the chiefs are the descendants of visitors from other lands.

Similar differences in custom between chiefs and their subjects are frequent in Africa, where again difference of custom is frequently combined with definite traditions of the descent of chiefs from foreigners, and the Incas of Peru were a conspicuous example of a similar process in America.[1]

[1] [See Perry, *The Growth of Civilization*, for a fuller development of this thesis.]

APPENDIX I

ON THE ORIGIN OF THE CLASSIFICATORY
SYSTEM OF RELATIONSHIPS

APPENDIX I

On the Origin of the Classificatory System of Relationships

Reprinted with permission of the Clarendon Press, Oxford, from Anthropological Essays presented to Edward Burnett Tylor in honour of his 75th Birthday, October 2, 1907.

LEWIS MORGAN is the only modern writer who has attempted to formulate a complete scheme of the evolution of the human family, a scheme based almost entirely on a study of the classificatory system of relationships of which he was the discoverer. According to this scheme human society has advanced from a state of complete promiscuity to one characterized by monogamy by a gradual evolution, the three chief stages of which Morgan called the consanguine, the Punaluan, and the monogamian families. In recent years the scheme has encountered much opposition, especially from Starcke,[1] Westermarck,[2] Crawley,[3] Andrew Lang,[4] and N. W. Thomas,[5] the last calling Morgan's whole structure a house of cards, and it may perhaps be said that the prevailing tendency in anthropology [6] is against any scheme which would derive human society from a state of promiscuity, whether complete or of that modified form to which the term group-marriage is usually applied.

---

[1] *The Primitive Family.* London, 1889. [2] *History of Human Marriage,* 3rd ed. 1901. [3] *The Mystic Rose.* London, 1902. [4] *Social Origins.* London, 1903, p. 90. [5] *Kinship Organizations and Group Marriage in Australia.* Cambridge, 1906. [6] The chief exception among those who have written on this subject in recent years is Kohler; see *Zur Urgeschichte der Ehe.* Stuttgart, 1897.

The opponents of Morgan have made no attempt to distinguish between different parts of his scheme, but having shown that certain of its features are unsatisfactory, they have condemned the whole. The elaborate scheme of Morgan can be divided into two distinct parts, one dealing with the existence of the consanguine family and the evolution from this of the Punaluan family, while the other part deals with the existence of this latter form of the family itself. It will be my object in this paper to point out a radical defect in the first part of Morgan's scheme, and then to endeavour to restate the second part of his scheme in accordance with the knowledge which has accumulated since his time.

The existence of both the consanguine and Punaluan families was deduced by Morgan from the characters of the classificatory system of relationships. This system is found throughout the whole of North America, and probably exists also in the South. It is universal throughout the Pacific—in Polynesia, Melanesia, New Guinea, and Australia. It is found in India, and some typical examples have been reported from Africa, over which continent it is probably very widely spread. Vestiges of it are found in other parts of the world, and it is probable that relationships have been expressed in this way by all the races of the world in the early stages of their development. The most important feature of the system is that large groups of people who, according to our ideas, are related in very different ways and in very different degrees are all ranged in the same category. The same name is given to a distant cousin once removed, for example, as is given to the father. On the other hand, relatives who are given the same name by most civilized people are in the classificatory system often rigorously distinguished. In this paper I propose to consider how far there is reason to believe that this system had its origin in the organization of early society, and especially in the early modes of relationship between men and women. In the first part of the paper I shall deal with the evidence provided by the system for the existence of Morgan's consanguine family, and in the second part shall consider the origin of the system in a condition of group-marriage.

THE NATURE OF MORGAN'S MALAYAN SYSTEM

Morgan's belief in the existence of the consanguine family, which corresponds to what is often called the undivided commune, was based entirely on the view that the variety of the classificatory system which he called Malayan [1] was the earliest form of the system. If it can be shown that the Malayan form represents a late stage in the development of the system, the whole evidence for the consanguine family falls to the ground so far as it is provided by the classificatory system, and Morgan himself acknowledged [2] that his hypothesis of the consanguine family rested principally, if not wholly, on this foundation.

Morgan supposed that the Polynesian societies which possessed the Malayan system were in a pristine state of culture, and he believed that their system of relationships revealed a corresponding primitive state of the evolution of the human family. We now know that Polynesian society is relatively highly developed, and it may perhaps be held to be superfluous to show that their kinship system, instead of being archaic as Morgan supposed, is a late product of change. I have been unable to find, however, that any student of the subject, whether supporter or opponent of Morgan, has refused to accept the Malayan form as primitive, and since the belief in its primitiveness is at the bottom of many of the difficulties in connexion with this subject, the evidence in favour of the lateness of the system may be given.

The special characteristic of the Malayan or Polynesian system is the small number of terms and the corresponding

[1] The actual examples on which Morgan based his Malayan system were from Polynesia, the name Malayan being chosen by him because he regarded the Polynesians as a branch of the Malayan family (*Ancient Society*, p. 403). In spite of much recent work on the Malays we are still almost wholly in the dark as to the kind of kinship system found among the different branches of that people.

[2] *Ancient Society*, pp. 385, 388, 402.

wide connotation of each. The same terms are used to denote relationships for which many different terms are found in most forms of the classificatory system ; thus, excluding differences dependent on age and sex, all the relatives of a speaker of the same generation as himself are addressed by the same name. The distinctions between father's brother and mother's brother and between father's sister and mother's sister which are usual in the classificatory system are not present, and there is a corresponding absence of distinctive names for their children. Morgan supposed that we had in this system the survival of a state of society in which all the members of a group corresponding to the brothers and sisters of a later stage intermarried indiscriminately, the consanguine family which he advanced as the earliest stage of human society.

I hope to show that this wide connotation of relationship terms is late, and not primitive, by pointing out that elsewhere we find examples where classificatory systems are undergoing changes which are modifying them in the direction of the Hawaiian form. My attention was directed to this problem by a study of the relationship systems of Torres Straits. We have in these islands two peoples in different conditions of social organization. In both there is patrilineal descent, with fairly definite evidence in one case at least that the people have emerged from a previous condition of mother-right, and the high degree of development of the idea of property would seem to indicate that their social condition is far from being of a primitive kind. On examining the social organization of the two communities we find additional evidence of their relatively advanced condition. The organization of the western islanders is totemic, probably in a relatively late stage, there being evidence of a previous dual organization which has become extinct. The social condition of the eastern islanders is probably still more advanced, having a territorial basis, with few traces of the conditions of mother-right and totemism from which they have nevertheless probably emerged. On studying the kinship system of these two peoples we find different stages of change in the direction of simplification. In the island of Mabuiag in the west the distinction between the children of father's brother and mother's brother is not present, and the name given to these relatives is also given to the children of father's sister and mother's sister. That the absence of the distinction is due to loss, and not to imperfect development, is rendered probable by the condition of the terms used for the older generation ; here there are still distinct terms for father's brother, mother's brother, father's sister and mother's sister, but there are definite signs that these distinctions are becoming blurred, and that the people are on their way to giving the same name to the relationships of father's sister and mother's sister, and possibly even to those of father's brother and mother's brother. In the Murray Islands in the east, on the other hand, there is still present the distinction between the children of father's brother and mother's brother ; but here the distinction between mother's sister and father's sister which seemed to be in process of disappearance in Mabuiag has completely gone. For the full evidence on these points I must refer to the articles on " Kinship " in the fifth and sixth volumes of the *Reports of the Cambridge Expedition to Torres Straits.* I can only say that the evidence is strongly in favour of the wide connotation of certain kinship terms in Torres Straits being a product of late change. These changes would not have to go very much further to produce kinship systems approaching very closely to that of Hawaii, and thus a strong supposition is raised in favour of the Polynesian system being also a product of late change.

If we now turn to Australian systems we find that it is universal, so far as the evidence goes, to have distinctive names for the four kinds of relative of the generation older than the speaker, viz. father and father's brother, mother's brother, father's sister, and mother and mother's sister. Similarly, in the next generation it seems to be almost universal, ignoring differences according to age, to have one designation for father's brother's children and mother's sister's children, and another designation for mother's brother's children and father's sister's children.

The only exception with which I have met is very instructive from the point of view which I am considering in this paper. The exception is found in the case of the Kurnai. In this tribe, which differs from all other Australian tribes in its mode of social organization, there are separate designations for father's brother, father's sister, mother's brother, and mother's sister, but in the next generation the corresponding distinctions are absent and the children of mother's brother and father's sister receive the same names as the children of father's brother and mother's sister.

In this respect the Kurnai system resembles that of the island of Mabuiag in Torres Straits while it retains the distinction between father's sister and mother's sister which has disappeared in Murray Island.

In one place [1] Howitt speaks of the Kurnai system as primitive, though two pages later he expresses doubts about this. The case seems to be very much like that of the Torres Straits people in that the social system of the Kurnai has a territorial basis with patrilineal descent, and few anthropologists would doubt that it represents a late stage in the evolution of Australian society. There can be equally little doubt that the special features of the kinship system of the Kurnai depend on loss of distinctions which once existed, rather than on a failure to develop distinctions found everywhere else in Australia.

If we accept the view that both the Kurnai and the people of Torres Straits show us late developments of social organization, we are confronted with the fact that in these relatively advanced societies we find variants of the classificatory system which bring them near to the Hawaiian form, though in none of the three has the generalization reached the degree present in that form.

---

[1] *Native Tribes of South-East Australia*, p. 168.

We now know that the people of Hawaii and other Polynesians are far more advanced in social culture than the inhabitants of either Torres Straits or Australia, and it seems an almost inevitable conclusion that the changes which have occurred in the less advanced peoples have in the more advanced peoples proceeded still further in the same direction, and have produced the system characterized by the extremely wide connotation of the relationship terms to which Morgan gave the name of Malayan.

If we now turn from these regions bordering on the Pacific Ocean to the islands of the Ocean itself, we find evidence pointing, I think, in the same direction. We find that the relationship systems of Fiji and Tonga possess the distinctions between father's brother and mother's brother and between father's sister and mother's sister, and they also possess the distinction between the children of father's brother and mother's sister on the one hand, and mother's brother and father's sister on the other hand. No one can have any doubt that the people of Fiji and Tonga are in a much more primitive stage of social evolution than the people of Hawaii, perhaps the most advanced of Polynesian societies, and though it is, of course, possible that the more developed society, so far as general culture is concerned, may have preserved a more pristine system of relationships, the association of highly developed general culture and a late form of relationship system is by far the more probable.

So far as I am aware, we have no accounts of the Hawaiian system other than that recorded by Morgan, but an account of the allied Maori system has recently been recorded by Elsdon Best,[1] and I think that any one who compares this account with those of the Torres Straits or Fiji can have very little doubt that we have in the former a later stage of the Papuan or Melanesian system. It would seem that just as the Polynesian languages have arisen by simplification of those of the Melanesian family, so have the Polynesian kinship systems

[1] *Journ. Anthrop. Instit.*, 1902, vol. xxxii, p. 185.

arisen by simplification of a variety resembling those found among Papuan and Melanesian peoples at the present time.

Lastly, let us go to Morgan's own people, the North American Indians. Among the systems recorded by Morgan himself we find some which approach the Malayan system. I will take only one example. An isolated band of Iroquois, called the Two Mountain Iroquois, had a form of the classificatory system in which the father's brother was distinguished from the mother's brother (though the two names are singularly alike) ; but the distinction between father's sister and mother's sister was not present, nor was any distinction made between the children of the father's brother, father's sister, mother's brother and mother's sister. Thus we have in the case of this Iroquois tribe a system which is rather nearer the Hawaiian system than that of either Mabuiag or Murray Island, each taken alone. If the definite loss which the Mabuiag system has undergone were combined with the loss which the Murray Island system has suffered, we should have before us a system almost identical with that of the Two Mountain Iroquois.

The Two Mountain Iroquois were colonists from the Mohawks and Oneidas who had settled above Montreal, and if their system is to be regarded as primitive, we have to suppose that this small band, who had apparently separated from the main body at no distant date, had preserved a primitive form, while the main body showed the usual features of the classificatory system. The system of the Two Mountain Iroquois was collected by Morgan himself, and we may therefore expect it to be accurate, and it is surprising that Morgan should have allowed this peculiar system to pass almost without notice, for more attention to it might have led him to revise his opinion that the Malayan form represents an early stage in the evolution of the classificatory system, and with the disappearance of the Malayan system as a primitive mode of expressing relationships would also have disappeared his sole evidence for the existence of the consanguine family.

The Origin of the Classificatory System in Group-Marriage

In the first part of this paper I have dealt with Morgan's evidence for the existence of the consanguine family, and I have shown that so far as the classificatory system of relationships is concerned we have no evidence for this form of the family. As I am not here concerned with the general problem of the existence or non-existence of this form of the family but only with the evidence for it derived from the classificatory system, I can pass on to the second part of Morgan's scheme, again premising that I have only to deal with the existence of the Punaluan family so far as the evidence for it is derived from the nature of the classificatory system.

By the Punaluan family Morgan meant a form of the family characterized by the existence of group-marriage, to use his own words, " founded upon the intermarriage of several sisters, own and collateral, with each other's husbands, in a group," and " on the intermarriage of several brothers, own and collateral, with each other's wives, in a group ". In each case he supposed that the spouses on one side need not necessarily be of kin to one another.

As Mr. Thomas has shown, the expression group-marriage has been used very loosely by recent writers, and it will perhaps conduce to clearness if we adopt Mr. Thomas's definition, though it does not correspond exactly with that of Morgan's. When I use the expression " group-marriage ", I shall therefore mean a marriage occurring in a community divided into definite groups, whether they be clans, classes, phratries, in which all the men of one group are the husbands of all the women of the other group, and all the women of the first group are the wives of the men of the second group. According to this definition all the husbands or wives would be related as members of the same group, and it is in this respect that the definition may differ from that of Morgan.

The arguments for the existence of group-marriage derived

from the classificatory system are briefly as follows. Often, but not by any means in all forms of the system, a man of one group will apply the same term to all the women of another group of a certain generation which he applies to his wife, and conversely all the women of one group may apply the same term to all the men of another group and of their own generation which they apply to their own individual husbands, and it has been argued that these terms are survivals of a state of society in which there were actual marital relations between those who used the terms. Secondly, a child of one group will give the same term to all the men of his father's group and generation which he applies to his own father, i.e. to all those who under the last heading would in some systems be called husbands by his mother, and it is supposed that this wide use of the term " father " is similarly a survival of a state of society in which all the men of a certain standing in the opposite group were his potential fathers. To this argument the objection is made that the child in all forms of the classificatory system gives the same name to the women of his own group and of the same generation as his mother as he gives to his own mother.

This objection to the value of the classificatory system as a test of previous social conditions was recognized by Darwin in his reference to the views of Morgan in *The Descent of Man*.[1] He remarks " that it seems almost incredible that the relationship of the child to its mother should ever be completely ignored, especially as the women in most savage tribes nurse their infants for a long time ". The objection still continues to influence many in their attitude towards the classificatory system, and the most recent writer on the subject, Mr. N. W. Thomas, has regarded the objection as a *reductio ad absurdum* of the hypothesis of group-marriage, and has jocularly commended such a belief in group-motherhood to the notice of zoologists.

Two quite different answers to the objection are possible. It may be that there was once a definite term for the individual

[1] 1871, vol. ii, p. 359.

relation between mother and child, and that the term became extended at a later stage of evolution so as to fall into line with other kinship terms. That such an extension of meaning can have taken place is summarily dismissed by Mr. Thomas as involving a process for which we have no evidence and for which no reason can be seen. As a matter of fact, however, as will be apparent from what I have said in the first part of this paper, people in low states of culture do extend the meaning of their kinship terms. Relatives once distinguished may come to receive the same appellation, and I see no reason to doubt that this process of generalization may have contributed to extend the connotation of the term " mother ". The other answer, however, probably presents more nearly the genesis of that generalized relationship which we have to translate by that of mother and child. In such a state of society as that we must assume when the system of relationships was in process of development, it is not probable that the special relationship between mother and child would have persisted beyond the time of weaning. Let us assume that the weaning did not take place till the child was three years old [1] and the separation would have occurred before the age at which the child began to learn the terms of relationship to any great extent. It is even possible that in this early stage of culture the duty of suckling may have been shared by other women of the group, and that, at the time of weaning, the child might not have been in the position to differentiate between its own mother and the other child-bearing women of the group.

To those unacquainted with society in low stages of culture it may seem very strange that a child should grow up without being able to distinguish his own mother from other women of his community. We know, however, that in relatively advanced societies with paternal descent, as in the Murray Islands, a man may grow up without knowing his real father and mother.

---

[1] I have assumed that weaning took place at this late age, because this now happens among many races of low culture, but if it was earlier, my argument is only strengthened.

In this case we have to do with adoption, and the case is therefore not parallel, but the occurrence of such ignorance in a relatively highly-developed community may help us to understand the absence of the knowledge of the personality of the mother at the much lower stages of social evolution which we have to assume at the time of origin of the classificatory system.

Again, the subject of adoption, which I have just mentioned, may throw some light on the matter. The people of the Murray Islands carry the custom of adoption to what seems to us an absurd extreme, and children are transferred from family to family in a way for which the people can give no adequate reason, nor can any adequate reason be found in the other features of the social or religious institutions of the people. I do not wish to go so far as to suggest that this custom of adoption may be a survival of a state of society in which children were largely common to the women of the group so far as nurture was concerned ; but this is possible, and in any case this wholesale adoption may help the civilized person to understand that people of low culture may have different ideas in connexion with parentage from those prevalent among ourselves, and that the idea of group-motherhood is not as absurd as Mr. Thomas supposes.

Only one other relationship term raises any serious difficulty, viz. the application of the same terms to all the children of the group which are applied to own brothers and sisters, but if my line of argument is accepted to explain " group-motherhood ", the existence of group-brotherhood and sisterhood will present no difficulty.

The point which I have considered is the most definitely formulated objection which has been brought against the value of the classificatory system as evidence in favour of group-marriage. The older objections [1] were based on the idea that the system is only a table of terms of address, a view which by no means removes the necessity for a theory of its origin. The

---

[1] McLennan, *Studies in Ancient History*, 1876, p. 366. See also Westermarck, op. cit., p. 89.

tendency of more recent objectors has been to show that the terms of the system are expressive of status and duties and not of consanguinity or affinity.[1] I shall return to this point later, and will only say now that the view that the classificatory system had its origin in group-marriage implies that it was in its origin expressive of status rather than of consanguinity and affinity.

Merely to reply to objections raised by others is, however, hardly satisfying. In the earlier part of my paper I have shown that we have reason to modify Morgan's scheme in a very fundamental respect, and it is now evidently necessary to restate the mode of the hypothetical origin of the classificatory system in a condition of group-marriage. Such a statement must be so highly problematical, and must involve so many doubtful features that I am very loath to undertake the task. I only do so because I believe it may assist clearness in the discussion of the problem if some definitely outlined scheme has been formulated which may make clear the points on which further evidence is required. My aim will be to suggest a state of society which would be capable of explaining the origin of the classificatory system of relationships, and at the same time is not in obvious conflict with what we know of man in low states of culture.

I shall have to begin by making certain assumptions. First, I assume that at the time the classificatory system had its origin, the custom of exogamy was already in existence, and, further, I assume, for the sake of simplicity, though it is not essential to my argument, that the community possessed only two exogamous sections, which I will call moieties. We now have so much evidence of such a dual division of early society that there are few who will object to this assumption, though my argument would apply equally well if there were more than two exogamous divisions of the community.

Further, I assume, again for convenience sake, that the child belongs to the division or moiety of its mother. This mode of

---

[1] Lang, *Social Origins*, p. 102 ; N. W. Thomas, op. cit., p. 123.

counting descent is again so widespread in communities of low culture that few will quarrel with this assumption. In the hypothetical community I assume we have therefore two moieties united in group-marriage, all the active men of one group being the husbands of all the child-bearing women of the other group. In each moiety four groups of people would be roughly distinguished ; the active men, the child-bearing women, the elders, and the children. The distinctions between these groups will be fairly clear except in one case. All that we know of savage society would lead us to expect that there would be a sharp distinction between the group of children and their seniors. The widespread ceremonies of initiation point to a time when there was a complete change of status at this period of life, and I assume that the change takes place at a definite time, i.e. that a boy does not become a man gradually as with us, but suddenly at the period of initiation. The distinction between child-bearing and older women would also present no difficulties, and the chief trouble in imagining the state of society I suggest arises in connexion with the distinction between the active men and the elders. If I may be allowed to pass over this difficulty for the present, we should find in such a society that a child would recognize in his community people who stand to him in eight different relations. In his own moiety there would be the group of child-bearing women to whom he would give a name which was the origin of that we now translate " mother ". Secondly, there would be the active men of his own moiety to whom he would give a name which later came to denote a relationship which we translate " mother's brother ". Thirdly, there would be the group of children to whom names would be given which later came to mean " brother " and " sister ". Lastly, there would be the group of elders whose names would have been the origin of the terms translated " grandfather " and " grandmother ". In the other moiety there would be four corresponding groups ; men to whom the child would give the name which we now translate "father"; the group whom he would call by the name which came to mean " father's sister " ; the children of the moiety to whom he would give a name which later came to denote the children of the mother's brother and father's sister ; and lastly there would be the group of elders who would probably receive the same names as the elders of his own moiety.

Such a state of society would give us the chief terms which we find. in the classificatory system, and new terms would be developed as the social organization became more complex.

In such a state of society I suppose that the status of a child would change when he becomes an adult, and that with this change of status there would be associated a change in the relationship in which he would stand to the members of the different groups. The great difficulty in the acceptance of my scheme is to see how the relationships set up by these age-groups developed into those regulated by generations such as we find among most people of low culture at the present time.

I cannot here attempt to follow out such a development in any detail, but I think it is possible to see the general lines on which one almost universal feature of the classificatory system may have evolved, viz. the distinction between elder and younger, especially frequent in the case of brothers and sisters. A man would probably tend to distinguish with some definiteness those who became adults earlier than himself from those who came later to this rank ; he would tend to distinguish sharply between those who helped in his initiatory ceremonies and those to whom he was himself one of the initiators, and this distinction between seniors and juniors would probably be carried over into the system of relationships which gradually developed as the group-relations developed into more individual relations between men and women, and as the society became organized into generations in the place of status- or age-groups.

There still exist in various parts of the world societies possessing age-grades,[1] which may well be survivals of some

---

[1] For a full account of these age-grades, see Schurtz, *Altersklassen und Männerbünde*, Berlin, 1902. Unfortunately, Schurtz complicates the problem connected with age-grades by including in this type of social organization the Australian matrimonial classes which have probably had an origin very different from that of true age-grades elsewhere.

such condition of social organization as that I suppose to have been the origin of the classificatory system. We have at present no evidence to show what relation there may be between these age-grades and the systems of relationships, but it is to be hoped that future investigation into the system of relationships of some community possessing age-grades may furnish material for the elucidation of the process by which the evolution from age-groups to generations has taken place.

What I suppose to have happened is that there were at first purely group-relationships which received names ; that from these named relationships the people were led to formulate certain further distinctions which reacted on the group-relationships and assisted in their conversion into relationships such as we find to characterize the classificatory system at the present time.

If I am right in the main lines of the sketch I have just given, the classificatory system was in its origin expressive entirely of status. The terms would stand for certain relations within the group to which only the vaguest ideas of consanguinity need have been attached. Several recent writers have urged that the classificatory system as we find it to-day is expressive of status only, and they have regarded this as a conclusive objection to Morgan's views. In the attacks made on Morgan's scheme during his lifetime the objections raised were of a different kind, being directed to show that the system was merely a collection of terms of address and had nothing to do with status and duties so far as status implied any function in the social economy. If Morgan were now alive I believe he would agree to a very great extent with those who regard the systems as expressions of status and duties so far as their origin is concerned, though his unfortunate error about the nature of the Malayan system prevented him from seeing to how great an extent the terms arose out of purely status relationships. It may be objected that he called the classificatory system one of consanguinity and affinity, but he called it this because, whatever may have been its origin, there is not the slightest doubt that at the present time the system is an expression of consanguinity and affinity to those who use it. I have now investigated the classificatory system in three communities,[1] and in all three it is perfectly clear that distinct ideas of consanguinity and affinity [2] are associated with the terms. The correct use of the terms was over and over again justified by reference to actual blood or marriage ties traceable in the genealogical records preserved by the people, though in other cases in which the terms were used they denoted merely membership of the same social group and could not be justified by distinct ties of blood or marriage relationship. There is in these three peoples definite evidence of the double nature of the classificatory system as an expression of status and of consanguinity, and there are definite indications of a mode of evolution of the systems by which they are coming to express status less and ties of consanguinity and affinity more.

The evidence relating to the classificatory system brought forward by most of the recent critics of Morgan has been derived chiefly from the Australians, and, so far as our existing evidence goes, it would seem that the status aspect of their systems is more prominent than in other parts of the world, as would be expected from the very special development of matrimonial classes among them ; but even in Australia it is probable that the aspect of the systems as expressions of consanguinity and affinity is far more important than the published accounts lead one to believe. The true relation between the classificatory system and the actual ties of blood and marriage relationship can only be properly brought out by a full application of the genealogical method, and this method has not yet been applied in Australia.

That there is sometimes a definite connexion between marriage regulations and the classificatory terms of relationship there can be no doubt. Thus I have shown elsewhere [3] that the

---

[1] Mabuiag and Murray Islands in Torres Straits, and the Todas in India.

[2] By consanguinity I mean blood relationship ; by affinity, marriage relationship.

[3] *Journ. Roy. Asiat. Soc.*, 1907, p. 611.

terms used by Dravidian peoples provide definite indications
of the marriage of cousins, which is a feature of their society :
and similarly there is an evident relation between the
classificatory terms and forms of marriage among the North
American Indians.[1]   When we find special features of the
classificatory system to have had their origin in special forms of
marriage, it becomes the more probable that its general features
are the survivals of some general form of marriage.

My object in this paper has been to support the view that the
features of the classificatory system of relationship, as we find
them at the present time, have arisen out of a state of group-
marriage, while pointing out that this system lends no support
to the view that the state of group-marriage was preceded
by one of wholly unregulated promiscuity. I should like again
to insist that it has not been my object to consider here the
problems involved in the growth of the human family in general,
but only to deal with the evidence provided by the classificatory
system of relationships.

The classificatory system, in one form or another, is spread so
widely over the world as to make it probable that it has had
its origin in some universal, or almost universal, stage of social
development, and I have attempted to indicate that the kind
of society which most readily accounts for its chief features is
one characterized by a form of marriage in which definite
groups of men are the husbands of definite groups of women.

---

[1] See Kohler, op. cit., p. 82.

APPENDIX II

SOCIAL ORGANIZATION IN AUSTRALIA

Social Organization in Australia

THE social organization of Australian tribes is of great theoretical importance. In this continent the dual grouping is frequent, but is usually associated with a complicated system of sub-grouping. Among some peoples, such as the Dieri of Central Australia, there are simply two moieties, with no sub-grouping. In other cases each moiety is again divided into two sections, leading to a division into four groups ; and elsewhere, again, there is a further process of subdivision, which produces eight sections. The chief, if not the only, function of these groups is the regulation of marriage, and in consequence they have generally been known as marriage classes, but Mr. A. R. Brown has suggested that when there are four groups, they shall be called sections, and when eight, subsections. Where there are only two moieties the regulation of marriage appears to be much of the same order as in Melanesia. A man must marry a woman of the other moiety, and within this moiety marriage is regulated by kinship, certain relatives being by social custom prescribed as consorts.

Where there is a fourfold division, there are variations in the nature of the rules by which marriage is regulated. A general similarity runs through all, in that a child does not belong to the group of either of its parents ; thus, if we call the four classes A, B, C, and D, the rules of descent will be as follows [1] :—

$$\text{If } A = b \text{ children are } C \text{ and } c$$
$$B = a \quad ,, \quad ,, \quad D \text{ and } d$$
$$C = d \quad ,, \quad ,, \quad A \text{ and } a$$
$$D = c \quad ,, \quad .,, \quad B \text{ and } b$$

[1] Capitals refer to men, small type to women.

Or, put in another way :—

It may be mentioned here that this scheme of regulation of marriage corresponds closely with that which would be produced by the cross-cousin marriage, and Mr. A. R. Brown[1] has found that, in tribes with the four-class system, the orthodox marriage is with the cross-cousin ; with the daughter of the actual mother's brother if possible ; if not, with the daughter of a classificatory mother's brother as determined by kinship, i.e. with one whom it is possible to trace genealogical relationship.

The eight-class system, such as is found among the Aranda, is more complex. In this system marriages take place according to the following scheme :—

[1] " Three Tribes of Western Australia " : *Journ. Roy. Anth. Inst.*, xliii, 1913, p. 143.

A. R. Brown has shown that this complicated system is correlated with, and he believes it to be the result of, a special form of marriage, in which a man marries his mother's mother's brother's daughter's daughter. Thus, if we take D in the above scheme, we see that his mother's mother's brother is E, whose daughter's daughter will be c, the wife of D according to the scheme. Again, the mother's mother's brother of A is H, whose daughter's daughter is to be the proper wife of A.

It is instructive to understand the process which a man goes through when he is selecting an orthodox bride for his son. For this purpose consider the arrangement of the marriage of D, which is done while D is still young, sometimes perhaps before he is born. His father will arrange who shall be his son's wife's mother : he cannot settle on the wife herself, because she may not yet be born. G goes to the mother's brother of his wife, that is E, and arranges that this man's daughter, namely b, perhaps not yet born, shall stand to his son in the relation called *nganji*. When D is born and grows up, he learns that b is his *nganji*, and that he will sooner or later marry her daughter, c, and does so when she is old enough.

Similarly, C will arrange with H, his wife's mother's brother, that his daughter, f, shall be the *nganji* of A, and A will subsequently marry b, the daughter of f.

According to A. R. Brown, the essential mechanism by which marriage is arranged in Australia is genealogical relationship or kinship. The marriage regulation takes two chief forms throughout Australia, one, the less frequent, in which a man marries his cross-cousin ; the other, in which he marries the daughter's daughter of the brother of his mother's mother. According to Brown, the marriage classes are nothing but systematizations of these two regulations of marriage by kinship, and the two rules are equally effective whether there are named marriage classes or not. Thus, he believes that such a tribe as the Dieri, who are stated to have only two moieties, with neither fourfold nor eightfold marriage classes, really possess these classes. He considers that they have not been named, and consequently have eluded observation.   Some Australian tribes group certain relatives together in classes with definite names, and refer to these classes when they are discussing marriageable and non-marriageable relations ; while other tribes discuss marriage solely in terms of genealogical relationship.   The marriage classes may be regarded as more or less concrete expressions of social ties, which can otherwise only be expressed by means of the nomenclature of relationship.

In this connexion A. R. Brown points out a fact which, so far as I am aware, had not been noted by previous observers, that a man cannot take every woman of the class into which he marries.   Thus, in the fourfold system, it will be noted that grandparents and children are in the same class, but marriage is limited to members of the marrying class of the same generation, and is not permitted with those members of the marrying class who are two generations removed, either in the ascending or descending line.

Mr. Brown's contributions to the better understanding of these complicated modes of grouping do not stop here.   He has found that, not only in West Australia, but also in other parts of the continent, the marriage classes co-exist with a local grouping.   The people who have a system of marriage classes are broken up into a large number of local groups.   In some cases the local group is exogamous, and in other cases not.   Where it is not exogamous, A. R. Brown proposes to call it a horde. Where it is exogamous he speaks of it as a clan, and this group corresponds not only with the clan or sib of the classification which I am using, but also with the territorial variety of the clan.

Where the local group is not exogamous, a child always belongs to the horde of its father, and this appears to be usually the case when the local group is exogamous.   Thus, in the schemes representing the nature of the four- and eight-class systems, it will be noted that a man always belongs to the same marriage class as his father's father.   In the case of the four-class system, Brown found definitely that members of the *A* and *C* classes belong to one local group, and members of the *B* and *D* classes to another local group, an association which necessarily follows from the patrilineal descent in the local group.

This definite connexion of descent with the local group greatly clarifies the situation which existed before the importance of the local group was shown by Brown. At one time discussions were frequent as to whether a given tribe was patrilineal or matrilineal, discussions which were largely beside the point, for they were carried out in reference to the marriage classes, and since, in the arrangement of these classes, a person does not belong to the group of either parent, these discussions had little meaning. If the marriage classes were the only groups which the Australian aborigines possessed, there would be no point in talking about descent at all. Mr. Brown has now shown, however, that the Australians have definite rules of descent, but that these apply to the local groups and not to the marriage classes.

I have so far spoken of the local groups as modes of territorial grouping. But, in general, each group has associated with it animals, plants, or other objects corresponding with the totems of other parts of the world. In other words, we have here a case in which the local clan grouping and the totemic clan grouping cover one another, so that we can correctly speak also of patrilineal descent of the totem. In some parts of Australia there is a totemic grouping which is not localized, and in these cases there is often matrilineal descent.

In dealing with the dual organization of Melanesia I pointed out that this organization extends over a large number of territorial units, which correspond with the tribes of our definition. In Australia the dual organization also extends over a number of social groups, which must be classed with clans; and it is possible that a more exact examination of the Melanesian evidence would reveal the presence of a similar form of local totemic grouping. We already have evidence in Melanesia of a totemic grouping within the dual organization, but we do not at present know of any case in which these totemic groups are localized.

There is reason to believe that, in Australia, the dual organization and the marriage classes are solely concerned in the regulation of marriage. Though they have attracted the attention of ethnologists, owing to their very unusual and complicated character, they are probably of small importance in the general regulation of life, as compared with the local and totemic groups.

It seems clear that, so far as political functions are concerned, the local group is the important unit, whether it be of the kind called by Brown a horde, or whether it be exogamous, and thus conform to the definition of a clan or sib. The exogamous group is also important in a religious, or perhaps more correctly, magico-religious respect, for in Australia the religious or magico-religious aspect of totemism is of great importance, rites being carried out by the totemic clan which are believed to increase the numbers of the totem animal or plant, and thus to augment the food supply. Owing to the great poverty of the material culture of the Australians, the economic aspect of its society is of little importance, but it is noteworthy that, in so far as it exists, it is closely bound up with totemism, and therefore with the local group.

Lastly, it must be noted that, in spite of the presence of two other forms of social grouping, the family, in the strict sense, is not only present, but is of great importance. It must be recognized, however, that the group called the family differs so much from that of our own society that A. R. Brown has found it necessary to give special definitions of the relationships which it involves. Thus, he defines a husband and wife as persons who live together, and whose union is recognized by the tribe. He defines a parent as a person with whom a child lives, who cares for him and provides him with food ; while brothers and sisters are persons who belong to the same family group. It will be noted that, in these definitions, Brown comes very near the definition of kinship proposed by Malinowski,[1] according to which persons are kin when they have certain duties and privileges in relation to one another. At the same time Brown makes it abundantly clear that, when an Australian is discussing social problems, the essential deciding factor is genealogy. The relationship of two persons to one another is made clear by an inquiry into genealogical relationships, though it may be that these genealogical relationships were determined in the first instance by such social functions as those by which Brown defines the relationships of parent and child, brother and sister, husband and wife.

[1] *The Family among the Australian Aborigines*, 1913, chap. vi.

APPENDIX III

THE DUAL ORGANIZATION

APPENDIX III

THE DUAL ORGANIZATION

THE work of Rivers has made it clear, once and for all, that the dual organization has played a part of fundamental importance in the formation of systems of relationship, and in the institution of marriages between relatives that play so conspicuous a part in these systems. He has shown (see pp. 51 et seq.) that many phenomena of social organization can only be explained on the basis of the former existence of a grouping in moieties between which intermarriage was the rule. In his work on *The History of Melanesian Society* he devoted much space to the consideration of the dual organization, and the reader is referred to that work for further details. He added much information to that given by Codrington in his work *The Melanesians*, and showed that the dual organization is of fundamental importance for the social organization of Melanesia.

Rivers was of the opinion that the dual organization of Melanesia came into being as the result of the intermixture of two distinct peoples, one of which migrated into the region and set up a social system in co-operation with the communities that they found there. He devotes chapter xxxviii of his work to that subject. He does not state that this must have been the origin of the dual organization, but says :—

" At the present time students of sociology are almost unanimous in ascribing the dual organization of society to a process of fission whereby a single social group came to be divided into two moieties. The opposite opinion that the dual organization came into being by a process of fusion has been put forward, but has few, if any, adherents. It has been my task in this book to show that many of the social institutions of Melanesia have come into being as the result of the inter-action of peoples and it will be quite in accordance with the rest of my argument that I should now attempt to show that the dual organization may have had a similar origin " (ii, 557).

He then proceeds to adduce the hostility between the moieties, the belief in physical and mental differences, certain incidents of mythology and so forth in support of his scheme. Thus, while making no positive statements with regard to the origin of the dual grouping, he marshals facts to support the thesis that it had its origin as the result of a process of fusion.

Another point in Rivers's treatment of the dual organization must be mentioned here. He tends in this book to distinguish the organization in totemic clans from the dual organization, while at the same time realizing that the two may be part and parcel of the same form of culture, as they certainly are in Australia and North America (ii, 83). While it is not possible to discuss the matter in detail here, it must be stated that the evidence for the dual organization as a whole throughout the world goes to show that this form of social organization is connected organically with the grouping in totemic clans, and therefore that any dissociation that occurs in Melanesia must be the result of some special circumstances in that region.

When Rivers wrote the lectures that are incorporated in this book, the subject of the dual organization had not yet received the treatment that it merited. Now that much fuller accounts of it have been published,[1] it is possible to view it from a wider standpoint, and to gain a juster notion of the part it has played in the social history of large parts of the world. The fact that Rivers realized so clearly the importance of the dual

[1] Cf. Perry, *The Children of the Sun*. London, 1923.

organization in his works on *Kinship and Social Organization* and *The History of Melanesian Society*, as well as in his article on " The Origin of the Classificatory System of Relationship ", makes it imperative to give a short sketch of the history of this form of social organization.

If we confine ourselves for the moment to India, Indonesia, Oceania, and North America, it can be shown with a great degree of probability that the earliest form of social organization beyond that of the food-gatherers, who went about in family groups, was the dual organization. But this dual organization was not so simple as would perhaps seem from the accounts given by Rivers, Codrington, and others. For it can be shown that the earliest food-producing culture throughout this vast region was essentially uniform, and that it represented a high degree of civilization, it being the result of a vast process of spread of culture that ultimately reached America. The social organization of this *Archaic Civilization*, as it may be termed, was the dual organization, together with a totemic clan system. Politically this society was of a highly complex nature. In the domain of material culture it has left its impress throughout this vast region by the installation of irrigation systems, often of vast extent ; by the building of monuments of stone, often of large stones, and often again conforming to certain types such as dolmens, stone circles and pyramids ; by the making of polished stone implements, and by mining activities, pearl-fishing and so forth. This civilization spread across the world as the result of the search for certain materials; gold, pearl-shell, pearls, copper, and other substances playing an important part in this activity; and as a consequence we find that the settlements of these men of the archaic civilization were made where supplies of these things existed in quantities. Thus it happens that practically every source of gold and pearl-shell from Egypt to America has been exploited in the past by men with this form of civilization.

In the region of Melanesia, where so much of the action of this book has taken place, there are valuable pearl-fisheries, in New Guinea, through the Solomons, in the New Hebrides, and off the coast of New Caledonia, there being also gold in New Caledonia. It is therefore a place where signs of the activities of these men of old would be expected. These signs are not lacking, for throughout Melanesia the material signs of the former presence of these men are forthcoming, especially in places with supplies of pearls and gold. At the present time in Ambrim, so often mentioned by Rivers, use is being made of dolmens ; in San Cristoval large stone mastaba-like monuments are constructed for the ruling groups, on top of which tombs dolmens are placed.[1] Stone circles are still in use in British New Guinea and the surrounding island groups.

To understand the real significance of the dual organization of Melanesia, Australia, North America, and elsewhere, it is imperative to appreciate the characteristics of this archaic civilization which lies behind every community of the food-gathering stage from one end of this region to the other.

The original settlements were possessed of a high degree of civilization, and were ruled over by definite ruling classes, entirely distinct in culture from the commoners. For instance, they practised mummification, while the commoners were practically universally interred in a contracted position. In the original settlements the ruling group was divided into two parts, one superior to the other, the superior part being led by the Children of the Sun, who are found from one end of the world to the other in connexion with the archaic civilization. The Children of the Sun were connected with the sky world, to which they went after death. The other side of the ruling group consisted of nobles, one of whom acted as a civil ruler of the state, and was in charge of warlike operations.

This part of the ruling group was connected with an underground land of the dead, as were the commoners. There was thus a bisection of the community at death, with the remarkable

---

[1] In *The Children of the Sun* I erroneously called these mastabas truncated pyramids.

distinction that, while the Children of the Sun went to the sky, the rest of the community, nobles included, went underground.

Not only was the ruling group of a community of the archaic civilization divided into two parts, but so was the land itself. This may well be illustrated by the first settlement made by the Children of the Sun in Samoa. They landed in the island of Tau in Manu'a, in the east end of the group. They divided the island into two parts, in one of which they lived, while in the other lived that part of the ruling group that was associated with the underworld. This dual division of the state was, so far as can be told, universal in communities of the archaic civilization. But it went much further than that ; for even villages were divided on the dual principle. In the island of Tau, just mentioned, the part of the island where lived the Children of the Sun had as its first settlement a village called Fitiuta, which was divided into Fitiuta-by-the-sea, and Fitiuta-landwards. This sea and land division of settlements is a widespread characteristic of dual communities, and it even extends to whole islands. In the Caroline Islands it is found that this dual characteristic of villages even applies to the landing-stages for boats, each part of the village having its own.

The two moieties in such dual communities have distinct characteristics, a point that has already been mentioned by Rivers himself. One part is superior to the other, the superior part being, of course, that corresponding to the one formerly ruled over by the Children of the Sun. The two parts are associated with the right and left hands respectively, and also with different colours. Hostility always exists between them, this hostility sometimes, as in New Guinea, expressing itself in chronic warfare.

It is necessary to explain how it comes about that communities so far apart in culture as those of the Australians and, say, early Samoa, can have acquired their culture from the same source. The explanation is simple. The Australians claim that the whole of their social organization was given to them by wonderful beings, usually connected with the sky, who came to them, usually from the north, organized them as communities with various rules and regulations, and then went away again. When these culture heroes are examined, in other places as well as in Australia, it is found that they move in the cultural atmosphere of the archaic civilization. In North America, for instance, the culture-heroes are practically invariably the Twin Children of the Sun. These beings are not fictitious, for the Children of the Sun were actually living in the United States after the arrival of Europeans. In like manner the peoples of Melanesia who have no ruling groups make a similar claim, and say, in Leper's Isle, for instance, that a culture-hero gave them their marriage regulations.

What has happened, therefore, in Australia, is that the ancestors of the existing Australian aborigines came into contact, in some way or other, with men of the archaic civilization, and got from them their social organization. This is easy to understand when it is mentioned that extensive gold-working and pearl-diving must have been prosecuted by these people in this region. In Melanesia, on the other hand, there are good reasons for believing that a ruling group formerly existed in places where now there is none. These ruling groups would have lived in the cultural atmosphere of the archaic civilization, with the dual organization running through the state from top to bottom. When they disappeared the communities would still retain their dual nature, at least for a time. So the existing Melanesians are similar to the right- and left-hand castes of Southern India ; they are the survivals of a former much more elaborate political system, the ruling groups of which have disappeared.

There is very little doubt that the communities of the archaic civilization took their character from the ruling group itself. This was dual, one part being the superior. What is more, there is good reason to believe that intermarriage was universally the rule between these two branches of the ruling group, for it actually goes on at the present time in the

Carolines, Timor, and elsewhere, and there are numerous traditional and mythological references to the practice. One very interesting feature of the marriage-relations between the two sides of the ruling group is that the Children of the Sun married their own sisters as well as women of the other side of the ruling group. So it would seem that the communities of the archaic civilization were ruled over by dual ruling groups which intermarried systematically, and imposed their rules of marriage on the rest of the community. In places where these ruling groups have disappeared the custom still persists among their former subjects as the exogamy between the moieties of the dual organization.

It must be noted that the dual organization of society just described is of a composite nature, including within itself elements of entirely different nature. In the first place there is the simple bisection of the community into two groups, which is a purely territorial division. Then, in addition, the ruling groups of dual communities are themselves dual in nature, and usually each part of the ruling group is associated with one side of the community, which side then takes its characteristic from the branch of the ruling group associated with it. The duality of such communities is not symmetrical; one of the rulers is a sacred king or chief, while the other is the civil king or chief. In addition we have the remarkable associations of one group with the sky and the other with the underworld. This asymmetry will have to be accounted for in any theory of the origin of the dual organization of society.

It is impossible to judge of the origin of any cultural element by itself; it must be put into its setting. So, when thinking of the origin of the dual organization, account must be taken of the fact that it was simply the social side of a civilization extending right across the world, and comprising many cultural elements. It is impossible, in America, Oceania, Indonesia, or India, to point to any facts indicating that the archaic civilization had its origin there. The only place where signs exist of the origin of this civilization is Egypt, and more than that, Egypt of the Pyramid age. Here can be watched the gradual assembly of the ingredients of the archaic civilization, which assumed its final shape in the Sixth Dynasty or thereabouts.

It has already been stated that the dual organization is composite in nature, and that it contains a duality of territory together with a duality of ruling groups, the two dualities apparently having little to do with each other. In Egypt of the First Dynasty the territorial duality—that which throughout the world expresses itself in a widespread group of communities in dual villages, islands, and so on—came into existence when the king of Upper Egypt conquered Lower Egypt. This happened about 3300 B.C., and henceforth Egypt was always referred to as Upper and Lower Egypt, the whole polity of the state being permeated with dual ideas resulting from the unification of the country under one throne. Thus, by this conquest there came into being in Egypt one aspect of the dual organization. But the country in the first four Dynasties was ruled over by only one king, and no signs whatever existed of the duality of the ruling groups such as characterize the communities of the archaic civilization. That was to come later.

The difference between the colour symbols of Upper and Lower Egypt, white being that of Upper Egypt and red that of Lower Egypt, was likewise carried across the world as a constant feature of the dual organization. The practices of mummification, of building stone monuments, of making polished stone implements, can likewise be shown to have been invented by the Egyptians, either in Egypt or in Nubia, and their addition to the cultural equipment of the archaic civilization is easy to demonstrate. The Egyptians had for many centuries previously practised irrigation, and all the settlements made as the result of Egyptian expeditions for materials of various sorts got food by this method. In the centuries succeeding the foundation of the First Dynasty the gradual taking shape of the archaic civilization can be watched proceeding step by step, until, at the time of the Sixth Dynasty, it was complete.

It was not until the Fifth Dynasty that the feature of the dual organization which is of interest in connexion with social organization came into being, namely, the duality in the ruling groups with the differentiation of sacred and civil rulers, connected respectively with the sky and the underworld. This second duality was superposed on the older territorial duality of the state by virtue of certain events that occurred in Egypt at the foundation of the Fifth Dynasty.

There is no particular reason why a dual community should be ruled over by two kings ; still less reason exists for the differentiation of function into sacred and secular ruler. How did this duality of rulers come into being in a country like Egypt, where territorial unification had already taken place under one ruler ? During the first four dynasties the king was the sole ruler of the country. His son, the crown prince, who was the vizier, carried on the administration of the realm One royal family, therefore, ruled over Upper and Lower Egypt. But at the beginning of the Fifth Dynasty there came into power the ruling family of Heliopolis, who called themselves the Children of the Sun. This is their first appearance in history. We now find that, throughout this and the next dynasty the viziership was held by members of another family, and that the crown prince never held that office. In the early part of the Fifth Dynasty it is probable that the viziers were men of very high rank who were connected with the old ruling group. Thus a duality in the ruling power of Egypt exactly similar to that characterizing the communities of the archaic civilization was produced when the Children of the Sun came into power. The original duality was the result of the fusion under one ruler of two geographical areas north and south : the second duality was the result of a fission in the ruling group, which occurred eight centuries or so after the former event. Towards the end of the Fifth Dynasty this system seems to have become firmly established, and, what is more, there seem to be definite signs of constant marriage between the ruling family of the Children of the Sun and the family of the viziers. Of course, it must be stated at once that the evidence is not yet ample, but what there is shows that the viziers married royal princesses, and the Pharoahs married, in addition, it is to be presumed, to their sisters or other near kin, women of viziers' families. Thus the two groups formed an intermarrying pair such as we find throughout the vast region from India to America. These intermarrying royal groups divided the domination between them, and doubtless entered on this compact of intermarriage in order to stabilize their position. This practice of forming matrimonial alliances between ruling groups can be observed in several places in the Old Testament as a recognized institution, which, seeing that the social and political institutions of the Israelites of that time were evidently permeated with Egyptian influences, is a sign of the intentions of the early Egyptian royal families. I shall return to this topic later.

It has been possible to advance one step further towards the assemblage of a social setting like that of the communities of the archaic civilization. We have found that the Egyptian ruling families became divided into two intermarrying groups with different functions. The associations of the two branches of the ruling group with the sky and the underworld can also be explained in Egypt. For the Children of the Sun were connected with a world in the sky where they went after death to enjoy the society of the sun-god. This form of belief was, in the beginning, confined to them ; the rest of the community went to the Osirian otherworld, which, in later times certainly was situated underground.

One more feature of the dual organization has yet to be accounted for, namely, the connexion between the two branches of the ruling group and the two territorial divisions of the state. So far in the survey of Egyptian history all that has been observed has been the foundation of a kingdom formed of the union of two distinct territories, and the bisection of the ruling group due to the coming into power of the Children of the Sun, who acted as sacred rulers, and left the secular administration of the country to members of other families. In the Fifth Dynasty there is no territorial distinction between the two parts of the ruling group, for both seem to have been associated with Lower Egypt or with the boundary between the two divisions of the country. But at the beginning of the Sixth Dynasty the family of the vizier appears to have belonged to Abydos in Upper Egypt, while the royal family lived at Memphis. Thus the two ruling groups belonged at that time to Upper and Lower Egypt, and in this way their resemblance to the ruling groups of Macassar, Samoa, and elsewhere is complete ; a duality in ruling groups has become completely superposed on a duality of a territorial nature, which superposition is characteristic of the dual organization of society in the archaic civilization.

Thus a series of historical happenings brought about the end of the Fifth Dynasty just that combination of features that characterize the archaic civilization in its earliest settlements throughout the world.

We have therefore, it seems, to assume that this civilization spread across the world, carrying with it all the essential details of the culture of Egypt at the time of the Pyramid Age, and especially of the Sixth Dynasty. In all the settlements, certainly those with ruling groups, the rulers imposed their characteristics on their followers. In most cases it seems certain that whole communities, with all grades of society, migrated from one home to another, and incorporated the native population among the lower orders ; so that social and political institutions would be transplanted by a perfectly natural and continuous process. Thus the marriage customs of the ruling groups, with the exception of the incestuous unions between members of the same family practised by the Children of the Sun, would be generally diffused throughout the community. Therefore the origin of the marriage systems of the peoples of Australia, Melanesia, Polynesia, North America,

India, and elsewhere must be sought in certain relationships set up in the ruling groups of the archaic civilization either before or after its spread from Egypt.

Although it can be shown with a great degree of probability that the scheme just outlined is correct, yet it by no means follows that the problems connected with the relationship systems of Melanesia and elsewhere are completely solved. Rather must it be said that we now know what the problems really are. We know that the sacred rulers of the archaic civilization practised incestuous unions, and that intermarriage took place between them and the other branch of the ruling group. We have a certain amount of evidence to show that the cross-cousin marriage was a feature of this early ruling group. This evidence is particularly clear in the case of the Bugi states of Southern Celebes, where both tradition and the early genealogical tables of the ruling families show that the cross-cousin marriage was the rule. This makes the ruling groups of the early Bugi states really one group of relatives, in spite of their different characteristics. The original stories tell of unions between people of the sky-world and those of the underworld, and they make it quite clear that these beings are intimately related; for the ruler of the underworld married the sister of the ruler of the sky-world, and vice versa. Therefore when the Bugi ruling groups carried on the same form of marriage in early times, it would seem that they were continuing the practice of former days.

If it were only necessary to account for the cross-cousin marriage the task would be simple. But complications set in when other forms of marriage are considered. What is to be said of marriage with the sister's daughter, on the one hand, and with the wife of the mother's brother, on the other, not to speak of marriages between persons who are two generations apart? How comes it that certain communities have adopted this form of marriage as the usual form of union, to the exclusion of all others, so that the relationship system reflects this union? The marriage systems of the Dieri of Australia and of the people of Pentecost in the New Hebrides reflect marriages between persons two generations apart, and these marriages actually were the rule. The puzzle is to understand how it came about that such marriages have become habitual.

MARRIAGES BETWEEN RELATIVES IN THE OLD TESTAMENT

It is probable that a brief account of the marriages recorded in the Old Testament, especially in the book of Genesis, may help the student to realize how that ruling groups may have impressed their marriages on the peoples among whom they settled. Unfortunately we lack information on this all-important topic from the region with which this book has mainly been concerned, and have to rely mainly on inferential evidence derived from tradition and mythology. I have found one instance, that of the ruling house of the Bugi state of Boni in Celebes, in which cross-cousin marriage was the rule in former times, but few such genealogical tables are available, so far as I am aware. In the book of Genesis, on the other hand, and throughout the Old Testament, there is a certain amount of evidence that bears on the points mentioned in this book, and especially in this Appendix.

In the first place it can be shown that marriage between relatives was considered to be all-important in the Old Testament. It can be shown without trouble that the posterity of Abram was royal. Abram himself was a king, and throughout his posterity emphasis is laid on their kingly nature : Esau, for instance, was the ancestor of the rulers over Edom.

When the marriages of this royal family are considered, it is evident that it was thought essential, for the maintenance of the royal blood, that marriages should take place between near kin. The table (p. 218) shows this.

Abram married Sarah, his half-sister ; Isaac married Rebekah, his father's brother's son's daughter ; Esau married his father's half-brother's daughter ; Lot was the ancestor of the Moabites and Ammonites by his two daughters ; Jacob married Leah and Rachel, the daughters of his mother's brother. Thus down through the royal line of Abram, Isaac, and Jacob the orthodox form of marriage was one with a near kin. It is to be noted that the marriage between Isaac and Rebekah was between relatives one generation apart ; and this also was the case in the marriage between Jacob and his cousins, if relationship be reckoned through Isaac instead of through Rebekah.

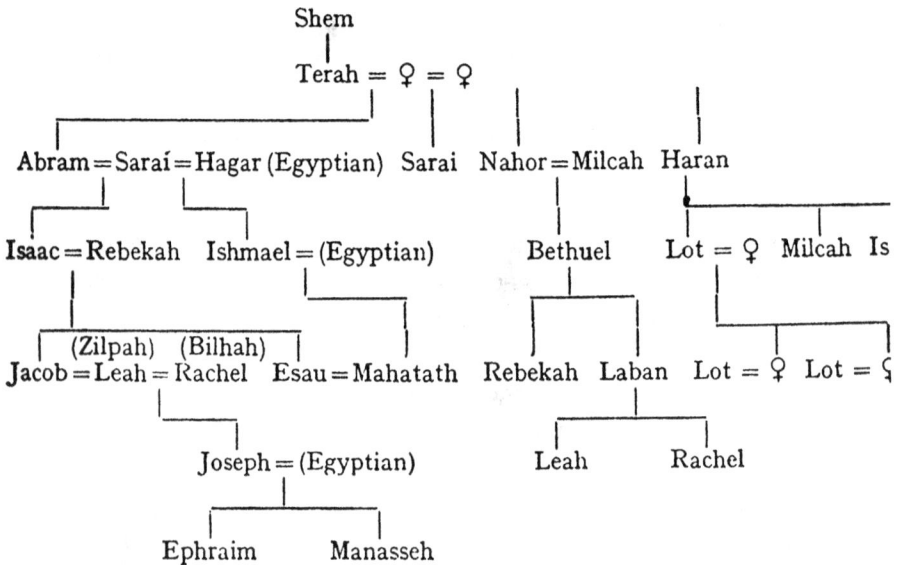

```
                          Shem
                           |
                  Terah = ♀ = ♀
  _____|    |        |              |
 |             |           |      |        |              |
Abram=Saraí=Hagar (Egyptian) Sarai  Nahor=Milcah  Haran
  ___|___     ___|___                   |        |_____
 |       |   |       |                Bethuel   |       |         |
Isaac=Rebekah  Ishmael = (Egyptian)       |    Lot = ♀  Milcah  Is
  |             ___|_____            __|__        _|_____
  |            |            |          |     |      |         |        |
 _|_ (Zilpah) (Bilhah) |    |         |     |     |        |       |
|  Jacob=Leah=Rachel  Esau=Mahatath  Rebekah Laban  Lot = ♀  Lot = ♀
        |_____                     __|__
                   |                    |     |
           Joseph = (Egyptian)        Leah   Rachel
           ____|____
          |         |
       Ephraim   Manasseh
```

The strong emphasis laid upon marriages between relatives in the case of the royal family is shown in the case of Esau. It is said that Esau lost his birthright and was supplanted by Jacob. What happened is shown by reading first of all the two verses at the end of chapter xxvi of Genesis :—

" And Esau was forty years old when he took to wife Judith the daughter of Beeri the Hittite, and Bathshemath the daughter of Elom the Hittite.

" Which were a grief of.mind unto Isaac and to Rebekah."

This shows clearly that Esau had offended in marrying women of other stock, or, rather, in not marrying women of his own. For Rebekah says in verse 46 of chapter xxvii :—

" I am weary of my life because of the daughters of Heth ; if Jacob take a wife of the daughters of Heth, such as these which are of the daughters of the land, what good shall my life do me ? "

Then follow some remarkable verses, where the story is continued.

" And Isaac called Jacob, and blessed him, and charged him, and said unto him, Thou shalt not take a wife of the daughters of Canaan.

" Arise, go to Padan-Aram to the house of Bethuel thy mother's father ; and take thee a wife from thence of the daughters of Laban thy mother's brother.

.   .   .   .

" When Esau saw that Isaac had blessed Jacob, and sent him away to Padan-Aram, to take him a wife from thence, and that as he blessed him he gave him a charge, saying, Thou shalt not take a wife of the daughters of Canaan.

" And that Jacob obeyed his father and his mother, and was gone to Padan-Aram.

" And Esau seeing that the daughters of Canaan pleased not Isaac his father ;

" Then went Esau unto Ishmael, and took unto the wives which he had Jahalath the daughter of Ishmael, Abram's son, the sister of Nebajoth, to be his wife."

The moral of this account is obvious. Esau had offended against the code by not marrying a near relative, and he was consequently superseded by Jacob, who, by marrying Leah and Rachel, his cousins, had kept the royal line intact. The descendants of Esau, like those of Ishmael, were the ancestors of ruling houses elsewhere, and not of the Israelites.

With this instance in mind, it is possible to understand how the ruling groups of the communities of the archaic civilization came to institute marriages between relatives as the proper form of marriage throughout the community. They considered it essential to marry near kin, and their followers acquired similar ideas. In the cases where the ruling group consisted of two intermarrying families, it follows that the cross-cousin marriage would be a normal form of marriage, and it would be thought that this marriage would be universal with the dual organization. But, as we have seen, marriages can take place between relatives one or even two generations apart, and instances of the first type are forthcoming in the Genesis table. Therefore it is possible to claim that the marriages between persons of different generations can well have arisen in communities with the dual organization as the result of such marriages in the ruling groups, but the exact mechanism determining the form of marriage in any case is not easy to suggest, and further information will have to be awaited.

It is possible to show also from the Old Testament that the practice of intermarriage was looked upon as a way of cementing the relationships between two groups. The first good instance of the sort is that of Dinah, daughter of Jacob, who was desired in marriage by Shechem, son of Hamor the Hivite. Hamor said to Jacob :—

" The soul of my son Shechem longeth for your daughter ; I pray you give her him to wife.

" And make ye marriages with us, and give us your daughters unto us, and take our daughters unto you.

" And ye shall dwell with us ; and the land shall be before you ; dwell and trade ye therein, and get you possession therein."

The speaker wished to cement the alliance between the two groups by intermarriage. The sons of Jacob answered him, and ended up by saying :—

" Then will we give our daughters unto you, and we will take your daughters unto us, and we will dwell with you, and we will become one people."

The habit of intermarrying with the Amorites, Canaanites, and others was a source of sore offence, and constant reference is made to it throughout the Old Testament. The vital importance of the avoidance of alliances of this sort is shown in

Ezra, where the great reform that was instituted at that time was the cessation of unions with other peoples.

" Now, when these things were done, the princes came to me, saying, The people of Israel, and the priests, and the Levites, have not separated themselves from the people of the lands, doing according to their abominations, even of the Canaanites, the Hittites, the Perrizites, the Jebusites, and Ammonites, the Moabites, the Egyptians, and the Amorites.

" For they have taken of their daughters for themselves, and for their sons ; so that the holy seed have mingled themselves with the people of those lands ; yea, the hand of the princes and rulers hath been chief in this trespass."

It goes on to say, in a later verse :—

" And now, O God, what shall we say after this ? for we have forsaken they commandments.

" Which thou hast commanded by thy servants, the people, saying, The land, unto which ye go to possess it, is an unclean land with the filthiness of the people of the lands, with their abominations, who have filled it from one end to the other with their uncleanness.

" Now therefore give not your daughters unto their sons, neither take their daughters unto your sons, nor seek their peace or their wealth for ever ; that ye may be strong, and eat the good of the land and leave it for an inheritance to your children for ever."

These quotations show that the Israelites were in the habit of contracting alliances with the peoples whom they found in Canaan, by means of intermarriage such as is found between the two sides of the dual organization. This therefore makes it probable that the Egyptian ruling groups had the same idea in mind when they began to intermarry, namely, that of cementing an alliance and of fortifying their position. And it is this alliance of two intermarrying families that was carried across the world as the foundation of the exogamy of the dual organization.

Further support for this view is to be obtained from the Old

Testament, where it can be shown that the Israelites from the beginning were in close touch with the Egyptians, and thus may have absorbed many of their ideas. Reference to the table on p. 218 shows that Abram, Ishmael and Joseph married Egyptian women, presumably princesses ; so did Solomon. It can likewise be shown that the political organization of Israel was permeated with dual ideas, the country itself being divided, in the time of the kings, into North and South, with distinct rulers, who at the same time, bear very similar names in several cases, such as Rehoboam and Jeroboam, Abijam and Abijah (who did not come to the throne of the northern kingdom), Asa and Baasha, Jehoash and Hehoash, all of which pairs were contemporaries. There is thus ample reason to believe that the Israelites got many of their ideas from the Egyptians, and that, consequently, their royal marriages and their matrimonial alliances are evidence of the customs obtaning in Egypt and of the motives which prompted the Egyptians to intermarry.

INDEX

THE HISTORY OF CIVILIZATION

Titles in the series

For Product Safety Concerns and Information please contact our EU
representative GPSR@taylorandfrancis.com
Taylor & Francis Verlag GmbH, Kaufingerstraße 24, 80331 München, Germany

www.ingramcontent.com/pod-product-compliance
Lightning Source LLC
Chambersburg PA
CBHW050428280326
41932CB00013BA/2029